GROWING
WOMEN
LEADERS

Nurturing women's leadership in the Church

ROSIE WARD

In memory of three leaders who died before their time:
Kathy, Fiona and Helena.

To my husband Malcolm, God's answer to my prayers;
you spur me on to be a better leader.

ACKNOWLEDGMENTS

This book has emerged from a long journey of reflection on women and leadership, which started in personal experience as a student leader, continued through theological college and into ordained ministry. Through that journey I've been particularly grateful for my theological training at Trinity College Bristol, where I began to engage with the nuances of New Testament text, early church history and feminist theology. The planning group of Men Women and God has been a great support and inspiration, and has stimulated my thinking; sometimes the stories I've heard of how women leaders have been treated have made me angry, and encouraged me to do more to help them.

Fiona helped me to admit to being a leader; Kathy urged me to keep writing; and Helena spurred me on to be myself. I'm grateful to them and to many other friends who have shared the leadership journey at various stages, and have helped to keep my passion for biblical equality burning brightly.

I'm so grateful to God, and to CPAS, for the opportunity to write this book. The Women as Leaders workshop at Cranfield helped me discover new perspectives. Thank you to Ellen Armstrong, David Banting, Susan Barter, Elizabeth Dyke, Jill Garrett, Ruth Hassall, Simon Ponsonby, Jane Stephenson and Malcolm Ward for reading the first draft and making such helpful comments; and to Rod Street who read chapter 1, and Shirley Jenner, Lorraine Purbrick and Kate King who read the section on mentoring. Because of you all, the book is very different from that early version. A double portion of thanks to my colleague James Lawrence, who read the manuscript not once but twice, and gave unstinting advice and suggestions. Thank you to Naomi Starkey for her enthusiasm for the project, and careful editing. My husband Malcolm is always an excellent critic, and has been patiently encouraging as I have spent hours writing and rewriting: thank you.

CONTENTS

Foreword 8

Introduction 9

Part 1: Women as leaders

Chapter 1   Interpreting scripture 20

Chapter 2   Leading women 51

Chapter 3   Telling stories 67

Part 2: Ways women lead

Chapter 4   A brief history of leadership..................................... 98

Chapter 5   Do women lead differently? 115

Part 3: Issues women face

Chapter 6   Power and service 138

Chapter 7   Building confidence and courage.......................... 154

Chapter 8   Stepping up to lead.. 172

Conclusion 204

Resource section 209

Notes.. 222

✣

FOREWORD

What does leadership look like? It is a question many people would answer by describing the public traits of great figures from politics, business, sport—even religion! But over recent decades, with the growth of interest in what it is about some leaders that makes their organizations great, some of our assumptions have been challenged.

No longer can leaders in any sphere deceive themselves into thinking that authority or influence can come from their position or status or from a 'command and control' approach. This is especially true in the Church. Although some parts of the Church may have the appearance of a distinct hierarchy, in practice they can rarely operate like that. The soft skills of leadership are indispensable.

The irony is that, although as churches we pride ourselves on our pastoral ministry, we have not always looked at church leadership through a relational lens, with the aim of releasing others to become the people God created them to be. This was such an integral part of Jesus' leadership that it is strange we might have missed it. Thankfully, though, it is being rediscovered. There are a number of reasons for this, but we cannot ignore the impact that women leaders have had. Whether by natural difference, experience or circumstance—all questions that Rosie Ward explores—women leaders have re-emphasized essential aspects of leadership. Leaders of both sexes are no longer constrained by 'masculine' or 'feminine' traits but are learning to integrate them.

However, cultural myths still abound about women leaders in the Church. There will always be theological debate about the appropriate role of women, but we need to get away from letting the inherited culture of churches shape our theological values. A book such as this, which explores our theology, history and psychology with the aim of releasing and growing women leaders, is a blessing to the Church.

+*Mike Hill, Bishop of Bristol*

✥

INTRODUCTION

'Service is the key form of life to any follower of Christ, and one of the many ways to serve is as a leader in the church.'[1]

For many Christians, having women as church leaders is now the norm. So why a book about women as leaders? Surely there are enough books on leadership around already? Yes, there are many books about leadership—over the last 20 years it has been a growth area—and there are a growing number of books about *Christian* leadership. But there is no avoiding the fact that we still live in a world where to be male has been normative and to be female has been different, derivative, secondary. That is true in society and it is certainly true in the Church. There is an expectation that leadership is male, so to some extent 'woman leader' and 'women in leadership' are oxymorons. Part of the aim of this book is to explore that paradox, that tension.

Many women find themselves called to lead but also hear competing claims:

- It says in the Bible that women should not be leaders.
- Women should not lead, because they are weaker and more gullible.
- We've never had women leaders in the Church, so why start now?
- How would you manage to be a proper wife and look after your children?
- Can women make the hard decisions of leadership? Can they 'do vision'?

Ever since a fellow student told me he could not be in my Bible study group because 'it says in the Bible that women can't lead', I've been passionate about finding out what God really says about women as leaders. To some people, that issue is yesterday's question; to others, it is very much alive and often painful.

IS LEADERSHIP MALE?

A couple of years after first hearing that women should not be leaders in the Church, I ran into the issue again. By this time, another woman and I were leading a Christian group for postgraduates in our university. Being forced to step down and allow a man (who thought we were doing a great job!) to take over the leadership was a profoundly painful experience. So we sat riveted to the words of Faith Forster and Pat Cook speaking at Spring Harvest in the early 1980s on women in leadership. At last—someone giving an alternative interpretation of the 'difficult passages' in the Bible and suggesting a whole different way of looking at scripture, tradition and the history of the Church.

When a friend and I went to talk to Faith, she recommended a book by Dorothy Pape, virtually the only book on the subject.[2] Since then, much has been published. By 1990, Gilbert Bilezikian had written *Beyond Sex Roles*, Mary Stewart Van Leeuwen had written *Gender and Grace*, and Gretchen Gaebelein Hull, *Equal to Serve*.

A variety of things warmed up the debate. It was the time when the Church of England was debating whether to open the priesthood to women, and there was a backlash against the emerging egalitarian viewpoint. The claim that women should be leaders was seen as a negative result of feminism—the Church following society. David Pawson wrote a book setting out his view—*Leadership is Male*—and this evoked published responses from Roger and Faith Forster, and Joan Martin. The Forsters published a series of articles, 'Is Leadership Male?' in *Renewal* magazine (1988), and Joan Martin compiled a collection of interviews with male leaders, published as *Is Leadership Male?* (1996).

WOMEN AS LEADERS

Much of the academic debate since then is summarized in Chapter 1 of this book. But while my bookshelves groan under the weight of books on women and ministry, there has been little discussion focusing specifically on leadership. Much of the debate has become focused, in the Church of England, on whether women can be priests or bishops (leaders of a particular kind). Many Christians now take women in leadership for granted, in the Church as in society, while others find themselves in churches that have created tighter rules to define what women can and cannot do. While we might have expected women to be increasingly free to move into leadership, there are churches where both men and women take a definite stance against women in certain leadership roles.

Some may wonder at a book on women in leadership when 'leadership' is not a biblical word. I am writing about leadership because, while it may not be a term found in the Bible, it is a thoroughly biblical concept. Many Christians recognize that leadership is a key to healthy, growing churches, hence the number of books and courses on 'leadership'. Leadership is also key to businesses and organizations. And while the actual words 'leader' and 'leadership' may be rare in the New Testament, an understanding of pastoral ministry as reflected in the life of Jesus and the teaching of Paul clearly includes leadership as part of it.

The Bible often uses the 'shepherd' metaphor for those who are to lead the flock of God's people. This word may imply a ministry of pastoral care but a closer look reveals that shepherd imagery refers to leadership more than to pastoral care. For example, the term 'shepherd' is often used in the Old Testament to refer to the political leaders of Israel. The psalmist tells us that David shepherded Israel with integrity of heart, and, in the parallel statement, 'with skilful hands he led them' (Psalm 78:72). In the New Testament, Jesus uses the same imagery when referring to his own leadership: 'I am the good shepherd... My sheep listen to my voice; I know them, and they follow me' (John 10:11, 27). 'Following' implies a leader. While pastoral ministry includes pastoral care, it must surely also include encouraging the mission of the Church, focusing the direction of the Church and developing other leaders, which are prime areas now encompassed by the word 'leadership'.

In addition, in many churches where the 'leader' of a local congregation is ordained or authorized, as 'pastor', 'minister' or 'priest/presbyter', while some pastoral or leadership tasks may be shared or delegated, that minister will be the main pastor, teacher, preacher *and* leader. Audrey Malphurs asserts that 'the congregation looks at the person behind the pulpit as the leader of the church whether or not it is true'.[3] Hence there is some focus in Chapter 1 on the debate about women preaching.

Jenny, a woman in ordained ministry, told me how her daughter, away at university, came home for the weekend with a friend. The daughter's friend belonged to a church where the congregation were taught that women are not permitted to preach or to be overall leaders in the Church. But she went to hear Jenny preach, out of respect for her hostess. Her response later: 'Your mum's a great preacher!' She had never heard a woman preach before, and her experience collided with what she had been taught and the assumptions she had made. While I do not wish to underestimate biblical argument, sometimes those who question women's leadership do so more out of ignorance and prejudice than thought-out conviction.

WHY THIS BOOK?

For most of recorded history, women have been largely excluded from formal leadership positions. If we think back to famous people in any sphere of life—political leaders, musicians, world rulers, scientists, dramatists, explorers, missionary leaders, religious leaders—the vast majority have been men. And while changes have been made, resulting in more women taking leadership roles in some areas of society, women remain dramatically underrepresented in formal leadership positions in politics, management, many professions—and the Church.

Alongside the dramatic changes that have taken place in the last 30 years, resulting in women's acceptance alongside men in almost all jobs and in other spheres—in sports like marathon running, cricket and football, for example—many of the old arguments about women being unfit for certain activities have worn thin. At the same time, there has been a surge in research about women as leaders, of most of which the Church seems unaware. Part of my aim in this book is to connect up Christian thinking about leadership with this research to see where it leads, while also drawing attention to the massive amount of recent research that affects how we think about women as leaders from a theological perspective.

Before women can step forward with confidence as leaders, they often have to navigate their way through all kinds of scepticism or downright opposition. In this book I want to encourage women to step up and lead—but sometimes they are able to do this only when the confusion of opposing voices has been cleared away.

One piece of recent research on women leaders in churches has found that they face a number of challenges that men do not face. For example:

- Women experience less encouragement than men to consider church leadership and often have fewer role models.
- They are more likely than men to choose ordained ministry as a second career, after a lengthy decision-making process.
- Women who start in assistant or associate positions are less likely to 'move up' to more senior church roles than are men (the so-called 'stained-glass ceiling').[4]

While this particular piece of research relates to Canadian churches, where there is in some places more resistance to women leaders than in the UK, it nevertheless resonates with anecdotal evidence from the Anglican Church and other denominations. Only God knows how many women are called and gifted but find themselves silenced by family, congregations or church leaders. Rachel felt called to ministry at the age of 17. She tried to explore this call within her local church but received no recognition, and she ended up going in a completely different direction. Yet the sense of call never went away. She finally found the courage to pursue it in middle age and started training for ordained ministry, at the same time being an advocate for other women.

CAREER AND LEARNING STYLES

Another reason for writing this book is to do with women's career development and the way their development needs as leaders are met. Susan Vinnicombe, Professor of Organizational Behaviour and Diversity at Cranfield School of Management, has suggested that women's development is different from that of men. She argues that the time when most men do their MBAs, in their 20s and 30s, is when women often have their most demanding responsibilities, so women may miss out. Some Christian leadership programmes are also targeted at this age group, sometimes making it more difficult for women to participate.

Vinnicombe has also noted four areas of tension for women in conventional leadership and management training, which have similar implications for women in church leadership. While I want to avoid gender stereotyping, these different tendencies are worth pondering:

- The centralization of authority and power in the classroom, which sometimes goes against women's preferred styles of learning.
- Reluctance among participants to admit uncertainty and ignorance; some women feel more able to be open in an all-women group.
- Learning by hearing about best practice rather than experientially; many women prefer the latter, although preference depends on personality as well as gender.

- Knowing through mastering analytical techniques rather than through emotional or intuitive connections; some women come to 'know' in more intuitive ways.

Many books and courses on Christian leadership take no special account of women's experience, or of the fact that men and women vary in learning styles. Most of the books on Christian leadership that I have read recently pay lip service to women in church leadership but include no examples of contemporary women leaders and few references to women in scripture or church history. This book aims to redress the balance.

READING THIS BOOK

I am convinced that women should step up to leadership in the Church not because of justice or equality, but because the Bible supports women in leadership. For me it is primarily a theological issue, a biblical issue. In addition, many of the challenges that women face as leaders would be solved if the Church was thoroughly convinced that they should take their place in leadership alongside men. Thus Part 1 of this book, 'Women as leaders', looks at issues of scripture and history, with chapters on scripture, women leaders in the Bible, and women leaders throughout the history of the Church.

Part 2 focuses on 'Ways women lead'; Chapter 4 is a brief excursion into the history of leadership and considers how to define leadership, aspects of leadership, and new directions in leadership. A key question, of interest to both men and women, is whether women lead differently from men. Behind this question lie centuries of debate on the 'nature' of women, and that is the subject of Chapter 5.

If it's true that God calls women as well as men to leadership, then how can they overcome some of the barriers they encounter?

There are particular issues that demand attention, and some of these are explored in Part 3: power and service (Chapter 6), confidence and courage (Chapter 7). I long for women whom God calls to be inspired to lead well, to continue to grow as leaders and to grow other women as leaders; Chapter 8 looks at a variety of other issues for women who are stepping up to lead and, in turn, looking to develop others as leaders.

I have not attempted to cover the subject of Christian women as leaders in professional or secular voluntary contexts; I hope, however, that much of this book may be relevant to Christian women wherever God calls them to use their gifts.

The book is designed to be read in order, but I have constructed each part so that it is relatively self-contained, and you could begin reading at any point. Each chapter ends with some questions, which could be used for personal reflection, discussion with a mentor or group discussion. At the end of the book there is a resource section, intended for reference.

Women in leadership is a huge topic. In this one book I cannot possibly cover everything I'd like to say. In particular, there are a vast number of books and scholarly articles relating to the theological debate about women as leaders, including some books that focus on a single verse. Thus my exploration in Chapter 1 is relatively brief but, I hope, gives a good feel for the main issues. Again, the resource section will be helpful; there are also endnotes, and further material is available on the website: www.cpas.org.uk/womeninleadership.

The book's focus on women in leadership is not intended to denigrate women (or men) who do not have this talent or gift and who exercise other ministries in other areas. My concern is that women who do have leadership talent and are called by God should be allowed to exercise their gifts, in a way that accords with the example of Jesus and the teaching of the Bible.

The issue of leadership in the Church—how it is to be done and, implicitly, by whom—is of concern to all Christians. I hope that this book will be of benefit to women who are leaders or aspire to be leaders, the women and men who encourage them, and all who are concerned for good leadership in the Church and long to see both men and women exercising their gift of leadership to God's glory and for the extension of his kingdom.

A NOTE ABOUT TERMINOLOGY

I am an Anglican, and inevitably know more about the Church of England than other churches, but have tried to embrace some of the debates going on in a variety of denominations and church groupings. Accordingly, I use the word 'minister' to mean clergy and other authorized or ordained leaders.

Discussions about women in leadership often employ terms such as 'egalitarian', 'complementarian' and 'hierarchical'. God created human beings male and female, and I believe that men and women are equal *and* complementary, but not that 'anatomy is destiny' (Freud). Such differences as may exist in physique, genes, hormones or brain anatomy do not necessarily mean that women are 'essentially' different from men in such a way that they are designed to fulfil different roles in society and the Church.

The word 'complementarian' is often used to refer to those who believe that men and women are equal in being but should have different 'roles' in society and the Church. Since this difference means in practice that, for example, men are to lead and women are designed to follow, many people would term this view 'hierarchical'. 'Egalitarian' is used not to imply that men and women are exactly the same in every way except obvious physical differences, but that both should be able to live according to their potential, truly 'complementary' to each other. Men and women are equally saved, equally Spirit-filled and equally sent, and women should not have to live according to rules made up by men, nor should they abdicate their responsibility for recognizing and stating their own needs. To avoid confusion, I have mainly avoided these shorthand terms.

As in social scientific writing, I have used 'sex' to refer to what is biologically given, and 'gender' when speaking about what seem to be learned or socialized differences between men and women. I use the word 'patriarchy' in its usual sense, to refer to a society in which power resides in male hands. It is now commonly acknowledged that patriarchy is deeply entrenched in most societies and pervades all major religions. The question at issue about patriarchy is whether it is 'inevitable' and part of God's design for his world, or whether it is the result of sin—an aspect of human society since the Fall—and therefore part of what should be reversed by the coming of Christ. I discuss this at various points in the book.

—— Part 1 ——

WOMEN AS LEADERS

Some women leaders wonder 'Should I be doing this at all?' Others are told, in one way or another, 'You may not lead.' I am convinced that many of the challenges that women face as leaders in the Church stem from the fundamental question of whether women *should* be leaders. Thus, this is the focus of Part 1. Chapter 1 looks at a variety of Bible passages which have been used to bar women from leadership, and the concepts of 'role' and 'headship', and explores wider issues of biblical interpretation and translation. Chapter 2 considers the question of women as leaders by giving an overview of women leaders in the Old and New Testaments. Many people are unaware of the number of women throughout church history who have been called to leadership roles in the Church, and Chapter 3 tells the stories of some of them.

✣

Chapter 1

INTERPRETING SCRIPTURE

'The heart of the debate pertains to the fundamental mystery of what it means to be a man or a woman.'[1]

As most readers of this book will know, the question of whether women should be leaders in the Church is a controversial one. Arguments based on scripture about why women should not lead have often held them back from Christian leadership. This is a huge issue and much ink has been spilt over the meaning of individual Greek words. However, little has been published in the last ten years at a popular level—hence this chapter, which draws on a wide range of recent scholarly material to build the case for women being leaders alongside men in the Church.

Anne Townsend, some of whose books I read as a young Christian, has written about the dilemmas of leadership for a woman from an evangelical background. She felt called by God and did what she could do—trained as a doctor and worked as a medical missionary. In her mid-40s she became editor of a Christian magazine and was then headhunted to be the national director of an evangelical charity, at a time when few women held public leadership positions in that constituency of the Church: 'Female leaders were dangerous, unscriptural creatures, who assumed "headship" over men. They were suspect.'[2]

While that was some years ago, a good many evangelical women still speak of struggles to discern whether their apparent calling to leadership is God's will or not. Some have the question decided for them: their church will not give them leadership experience, use their gifts fully, encourage them towards further training, or employ them as leaders if they do become accredited or authorized.

WOMEN PRIESTS, WOMEN PREACHERS?

There are several different but related issues that result in women being denied a variety of leadership roles.

- For some evangelicals, women should not teach or preach (usually, not teach or preach to mixed gatherings of adults) because they believe that this contravenes Paul's teaching in 1 Corinthians 14:34–35 and 1 Timothy 2:12. Theoretically such women could be leaders but, where the central event of the gathered church community is preaching, it is difficult for someone who cannot preach to be a leader.
- Others argue that women can teach but cannot be overall leaders: the so-called 'headship' issue. They affirm women's ministry but want to avoid going against this scriptural principle.
- Others argue a variation of this point, that men and women are equal but different, with part of this difference being that they have different God-given roles: 'A man, just by virtue of his manhood, is called to lead for God. A woman, just by virtue of her womanhood, is called to help for God.'[3] Where the lines are drawn in relation to church leadership varies considerably in practice.
- Some appeal to the Trinity, arguing that women's permanent subordination to men from creation reflects the subordination of Jesus to the Father.
- In churches where tradition carries as much weight as or more than scripture, the fact that there have never been women in leadership positions is given as an argument for not acting differently now.
- In the Catholic wing of the Church, including parts of the Church of England, some believe that a woman cannot represent Christ and so cannot be a priest. Since most priests are leaders of congregations, this effectively bars women from leadership in local churches.

While some of those who see the Bible as placing restrictions on women's leadership argue that women gifted with leadership ability are encouraged to take on leadership responsibilities within a proper 'ordering', or appropriate 'roles', this is often difficult to put into practice. All too often, such well-meaning restrictions have the following consequences:

- Able women who are emerging leaders receive mixed messages.
- Language of 'appropriate difference' ends up as implying inferiority: women ministers are barred from some areas of ministry, only to be treated more like secretaries or restricted to work with other women.
- Ironically, some women will find that they are more free to minister in other churches without theological objections to their leadership, and may leave in order to use their gifts rather than face the battles in their home churches.

PRINCIPLES OF INTERPRETATION

How not to decide

How should we decide what is the God-given nature of women, and what God intends for women? The deepest questions of theology and practice are not answered exclusively by exegesis (the interpretation of biblical texts), although most of this chapter looks closely at a number of disputed texts. John Stackhouse has helpfully suggested that the task of theology is to 'formulate an interpretation that does the best job, relative to other options, of explaining most of the most important data and as much of the remainder as possible'.[4] Anglicans have long employed scripture, tradition and reason; experience, too, must play a part, not in going against scripture but sometimes in helping us to look afresh at what the Bible actually says.

If we are sincerely looking for a biblical perspective on women in leadership, we do not go far before discovering that there are complex matters of language, culture and interpretation involved, a history of the debate to draw upon—the experience of previous interpreters—and our own prejudices and preconceptions to examine before we can hope to arrive at a decision.

It is worth mentioning a couple of other ways in which people make up their minds about this issue: culture and intuition. Some take today's culture as the norm and support women's leadership in the Church because 'society says' that women can and should lead. But society cannot be assumed to be either right or wrong.

Many women who have felt called to a ministry of preaching or leadership in the Church have relied on their intuition or sense of the Spirit's leading: 'the Spirit says so'. Relying only on intuition can be dangerous; ideally a sense of call combines the subjective inner call and the Church's confirmation of it. In the past, many women did great things for God through obeying what they believed to be his call, despite the Church's attitude to them. Now, however, they should not have to pit their sense of calling against church teaching, when the two should work together. I believe passionately that God's plan has always been for women and men to work together to lead his Church.

'Control texts?'

In the past, some have argued from 'control texts'. For example, one key control text for egalitarians has been Galatians 3:28, used by women and men to defend women's public ministry past and present. The problem with this is that others can pose another control text in response—1 Corinthians 14:34, for example.

Galatians 3:28 suffers badly from mistranslation. We usually read, 'There is neither Jew nor Gentile, neither slave nor free, neither male nor female, for you are all one in Christ Jesus' (so TNIV). Paul uses a different word in the third couplet, however, such that it should read 'no male *and* female'. Tom Wright suggests that Paul is quoting Genesis 1:27 ('male and female he created them') as part of his argument in Galatians that males are no longer privileged, thus circumcision is irrelevant. Thus, Galatians 3:28 emphasizes equality for believers but also challenged the Gnostic propensity to flatten all male–female distinctions by effectively turning women into men.[5] The verse may have long served as a useful shorthand for equality, but we now need to use better arguments than this.

There is a growing consensus that it is important to seek an answer based on the whole trajectory of scripture, and not focus solely on key passages that have resulted in a spiritual slanging match over the last 20–30 years. I want to take a wider view, which includes issues of translation, interpretation and overarching assumptions as much as it concerns individual texts.

Hermeneutical principles

Although individual texts can only take us so far in establishing the case for women leaders in the Church, it is clearly essential to interpret such verses as fully as possible. As we wrestle with these so-called 'difficult passages', it is helpful to keep in mind the following principles for interpretation:

- The Bible is the word of God, and thus we expect to find consistency. One passage of scripture should not be interpreted in such a way as to contradict other passages or the broad sweep of scripture.
- Priority must be given to clear and unambiguous passages over difficult and obscure ones, but the latter must not be ignored.
- Narrative and propositional statements must be interpreted in the light of each other. The type of writing involved must be considered—letters, for example.
- Interpretations must take account of the background and cultural context.
- We need to be aware of our own presuppositions and how they may influence our interpretation.

- Any interpretation should build on previous work but tradition is not sacrosanct. Any current interpretation may be challenged in the light of new understandings of language, culture or other relevant evidence.
- Application based on any interpretation has to consider how a biblical situation relates to a situation today, and whether a command or practice applied only to its original context or is of permanent and unvarying application.
- We also need to consider whether (in this case) the leadership of women is a doctrine of first order importance or whether it is one where churches may interpret the Bible differently and therefore vary in practice (as in church order, baptism, politics and so on).

The significance of translation

The Bible translations that we read affect our interpretations (in places, crucially) when they themselves depend on prior theological questions. Languages do not have a one-to-one relationship to another, as most of us discovered at school when trying to translate French or German. Language structures differ, and there are some inadequacies of language; for example, English has 'his/her' in the singular but only one plural ('they') for men, women or both. Changes have taken place in English usage such that 'man' meaning both man and woman is no longer the norm, and 'men' is now assumed to mean 'male people'.

We cannot ignore this shift if we want to communicate meaningfully. For example, if the word 'brothers' is used to translate *adelphoi* when, as Howard Marshall has argued,[6] Paul was addressing mixed groups, then we are misleading our readers. The correct translation of *adelphoi* is normally 'brothers and sisters', except where the context requires otherwise. To use only 'brothers' suggests (unintentionally or perhaps intentionally) that some of Paul's teaching about discipleship and leadership was addressed only to men.

All biblical translators are influenced not only by their cultural presuppositions but also, often, by theological understanding. This in turn influences the translation of particular words or phrases, which in turn again influences how readers form their theology from what they read. Hence, faulty theology can be based on mistranslation. Here are some examples of how different translations of various words and phrases related to women's ministry have far-reaching implications.

Was Phoebe a servant or a leader ?

In Romans 16:1–2, Phoebe is described as a *diakonos* of the church at Cenchreae. *Diakonos* can mean 'servant' but it is a masculine word not normally applied to female servants. Consider the difference in implication between the word 'servant' (used in NIV and KJV) and 'deaconess' (RSV), 'deacon' (NRSV and TNIV) or one 'who holds office' (NEB).

Can women pass on Paul's teaching to others?

2 Timothy 2:2 says, 'The things you have heard me say in the presence of many witnesses entrust to reliable *men* who will also be qualified to teach others' (NIV). Paul uses the word *anthropos* here, which could refer to humanity in general, or to a group of men and women, or to a group of men. If Paul clearly intended a group of men, he could have used the word *aner*. Hence NRSV translates, '… entrust to faithful *people*', which leaves it open for this question to be decided on the basis of other texts.

Women deacons?

1 Timothy 3:8–12 lists the qualifications for deacons, but who are the 'women' in verse 11? The TNIV reads, 'In the same way the women are to be worthy of respect', with a footnote to *women* which

reads 'Probably women who are deacons'. There is good linguistic evidence for translating the Greek *gyne* as 'woman' rather than 'wife' here, yet many translations use 'wife', taking it for granted that it is deacons' wives who are referred to.

The rest of this chapter focuses on two passages of scripture commonly used to restrict women's speaking ministry, before going on to look at issues around 'headship' and role subordination, which are held by some to rule out women as leaders.

1 TIMOTHY 2:11–15

A friend of mine had preached at her (Baptist) church. A woman came up to her as she stood at the door and shook her hand: 'That was really anointed, the most anointed preaching I've heard for a long time.' The woman went on to explain why the sermon had helped her, but finished, 'I've just one problem—I don't agree with women preachers.'

1 Timothy 2:11–15 has been described as 'the single most effective weapon to keep women from active and equal participation in the church'. Since I cited this comment in my book on women in evangelism published in 1987, arguments have moved on. Over the last ten years there has been considerable scholarly attention given to these verses, and an increasing consensus has emerged that, correctly interpreted, what Paul wrote was not intended to bar women permanently from teaching or leadership.

This is the only passage in the Bible that is unambiguously about women teaching and leading, but, according to John Stott,[7] these are probably the most controversial verses in the pastoral epistles, with four obscure words and numerous other difficulties.

Many Christians are used to reading these verses as translated in the NIV:

A woman should learn in quietness and full submission. I do not permit a woman to teach or to have authority over a man; she must be silent. For Adam was formed first, then Eve. And Adam was not the one deceived; it was the woman who was deceived and became a sinner. But women will be saved through childbearing—if they continue in faith, love and holiness with propriety.

The meaning may seem obvious, yet, even when read at face value, the passage is highly problematic. For example, if women are not permitted to teach men, why do many Christian men value books written by women? Again, the idea that 'women will be saved through childbearing' directly contradicts the belief that we are saved through the death of Christ. Clearly some interpretation is needed. The question is, which interpretation best fits the text and the context, and makes sense of the whole passage, not just a couple of verses?

I would like to propose the following as a more accurate translation, for reasons that I will explain:

Let a woman learn undisturbed, in full submission to God. I am not saying that a woman should teach in a domineering way, but she should have a quiet demeanour. For Adam was created first, then Eve. And Adam was not deceived but the woman was deceived, and fell into sin. She will, however, be kept safe through the process of childbirth, if she remains in faith, love and holiness with self-control.

Translation, translation

One key issue here is translation; if we cannot read New Testament Greek, we are likely to be most influenced by our favourite Bible version. Most of us are used to verse 12 reading, 'I do not permit a woman to teach or to have [or *exercise*] authority over a man.' This was the version quoted to me when I was a student, in the incident I described in the Introduction.

Interestingly, translations dating from before the 1940s normally translated the word *authentein* as 'to dominate' rather than 'to have authority over'. For example, the Latin Vulgate (fourth to fifth century) reads 'neither to domineer over a man' and the King James Bible (1611) 'I suffer not a woman to teach, nor to *usurp* authority over a man.' Belleville[8] gives numerous other examples.

Might one conclusion be that post-1940s translation has been influenced by those who wanted to see women excluded from leadership? It is arguable that after the World Wars, women were moving into the 'male' working world, and a backlash against women's leadership started around this time. Nowhere else in Paul's letter is there any direct discussion of the sex of leaders, but only of their spiritual qualifications for leadership.

Much work has been done on this text in recent years, and this is reflected in the TNIV's footnotes to verse 12 ('I do not permit a woman to teach or to assume authority over a man; she must be quiet'): 'Or *teach a man in a domineering way*; or *teach or to exercise* (or *have*) *authority over a man'*; a second footnote to the word 'man' says 'Or *over her husband'*. This at least alerts readers to alternative readings, which make for alternative interpretations.

The Greek word *authentein* is notoriously difficult to translate because this is the only use of it in the New Testament, and usage elsewhere has a variety of meanings. The most common meaning of the noun *authentes*, by the first century, was 'the perpetrator of a murder committed by others'. Verb forms are rare, but most common are the meanings 'to control, restrain, dominate, gain the upper hand'. There is thus no lexical warrant for translating the word 'to exercise authority over'; this meaning did not appear until several centuries later.

So how did 'exercise authority over' gain such wide acceptance in translation and by some scholars? The issues are complicated but are partly to do with the grammatical expression and its relation to the phrase about teaching. However, it is more in keeping with grammatical sense and with its meaning to translate the whole phrase, 'I do not permit a woman to teach a man in a domineering way but to have a quiet demeanour' (literally, 'to be in calmness').[9]

Cultural context?

Taking the context of a passage into account is important. If we try to read and apply every word of scripture directly to ourselves, we will realize that we are all selective. We cannot say that 1 Timothy 2:9, about women adorning themselves 'not with elaborate hairstyles or gold or pearls or expensive clothes', applied only to the women of Ephesus, while verse 11 applies directly to us. (I have never heard women taught that they, unlike men, are not to wear gold wedding rings.)

If women are not to teach in a domineering way, the next question that follows is, why should women have been behaving like this in Ephesus at the time? Over the last couple of decades we have gained a much greater understanding of the background to the New Testament and its writings than earlier scholars possessed. One possible reason that women might have been tempted to domineer is the influence of the cult of Artemis, in which women were considered superior to men. There is evidence of high priestesses in the area around Ephesus, where Timothy was living when Paul wrote this letter to him.

A more fruitful way of interpreting these difficult verses may thus be to take account of the wider context. There clearly were false teachers around. As Linda Belleville argues, 'If the Ephesian women were being encouraged as the superior sex to assume the role of teacher over men, this would go a long way toward explaining 1 Timothy 2:3–14.'[10] These surrounding verses are often ignored in the narrow focus on verses 11–12. Paul is, then, prohibiting only teaching that tries to get the upper hand—not teaching per se.

Women must learn

A similar interpretation of these verses has been offered by the New Testament scholar Tom Wright. He offers his own translation of verses 11–12 as follows: 'They [women] must be allowed to study undisturbed, in full submission to God. I'm not saying that women should try to teach men, or dictate to them; rather, that they should be left undisturbed.'[11]

Wright draws on the same increased understanding of cultural background, and he also goes beyond the usual arguments. Just as, when out cycling, I can put on dark glasses or yellow glasses and see things quite differently, so, if we try to approach this passage without our previous assumptions, we can see things afresh.

Paul says that women should *learn* (v. 11). Until that time, women had been very much in the background in their religious as well as social culture: now Paul wants them to catch up, and that means they need to learn. Wright then suggests that the word for 'submission', which grammatically has no object but has been assumed to be 'men' or their husbands, should more logically relate to God (which would be true for men as well).

Verse 12 is then a caveat relating to the presence of priestesses. To write that women needed to study, learn and take a leadership role, in the context of the Artemis cult, might have been seen as encouraging women to behave like those in the cult, and would give Christianity a bad name. So Paul says, 'I don't mean to imply that I'm setting up women as the new authority over men in the same way that men previously held authority over women.'[12] Wright thus takes a similar line to Belleville in translating *authentein* as 'try to dictate to'—with overtones of 'be bossy' or 'seize control'.

What is the point of the reference to Adam and Eve? That Adam was created before Eve (v. 13) is stated in Genesis 2, but this does not make it a principle.[13] Wright argues that the emphasis in verse 14 is on the need to learn so as not to be deceived: 'Look what happened when Eve was deceived. Women need to learn just as much as men do.'[14] And childbirth (v. 15)? Verse 15 clearly cannot be taken at face value. Women are not saved through bearing children. According to Wright, Paul offers the assurance that bearing a child may be hard but it is not meant to be a sign of God's displeasure. Other scholars suggest that this childbearing reference may be a rebuttal of false teachers who discouraged marriage, or that it may refer to salvation through the birth of Christ ('the Childbearing').[15] If it is a refutation of heretical teaching about marriage, this may make it easier to interpret verses 13–14, which would then allude to the same heretical teaching—that Eve was created first and that she was not deceived. Paul is thus putting the record straight by recounting what really happened.

These verses should encourage all of us to use our God-given gifts. Women and men both need to learn about God. That needed saying in the first century, and, in a context where women still sometimes rely on their husbands for spiritual advice, I believe that Paul would exhort those women today to learn for themselves. While there remains a lack of clarity about these verses, there is nonetheless a good consensus. Paul rules out any kind of domineering, bossy teaching, or teaching that sets one sex over another. What he does not do is rule out teaching or any other kind of ministry by women.

Many interpreters have looked back to early Bible commentators, who were often influenced by their own presuppositions and prejudices. On this passage, Tertullian wrote in a treatise *On the Dress of Women* (c.200): '*You* are the devil's gateway: *you* are the unsealer of that (forbidden) tree... *You* destroyed so easily God's image, man.'[16] Chrysostom (writing in the early fourth century) set the tone for later theologians: 'She taught the man once, upset everything, and made him liable to disobedience... therefore he [Paul] says, "let her not teach".'[17]

It is time once and for all to break free from this legacy of false teaching, which stems ultimately from the idea that women are by nature inferior to men. Instead of proclaiming a radical new way of being men and women, we have in the Church all too often perpetuated the cycle of domination and suppression that was introduced at the Fall. It is time for a change, and for the Church at last to be at the forefront of ending the battle of the sexes

1 CORINTHIANS 14:33-35

This passage is about women speaking rather than leading, but it is so often connected to 1 Timothy 2:11–12 that I will deal with it briefly here. The NIV translates as follows:

For God is not a God of disorder but of peace. As in all the congregations of the saints, women should remain silent in the churches. They are not allowed to speak, but must be in submission, as the Law says. If they want to enquire about something, they should ask their own husbands at home; for it is disgraceful for a woman to speak in the church.

Very few people take 'women should remain silent in the churches' at face value. I do not know of any churches where women are not allowed to sing, for example, or to greet their Christian brothers and sisters informally. The instructions in 1 Corinthians 11 about how women should be dressed when they are taking part in worship would not be necessary if they were silent all the time. So the question is, what sort of silence was Paul advocating, and what sort of speaking were they not allowed to do?

Possible interpretations

The following list of possible interpretations which have been offered in recent years is derived from the book by Craig Keener, *Paul, Women and Wives*.[18] Keener makes a more recent contribution to the debate in a chapter on this passage in *Discovering Biblical Equality.*[19]

- Some scholars have argued that verses 34–35 are a later addition to the passage. This has become quite a reputable and widespread view, but the evidence for it is limited and most Christians with a high view of scripture accept the Bible as we have received it.
- The verses could be a quotation from Paul's opponents, which he is refuting. This is unlikely.
- Worship was segregated, so women were calling out to their husbands across a divide, making the worship noisy. However, there is no evidence that synagogues were segregated in this period and, in any case, the Corinthian church met in homes.
- The passage is about the abuse of gifts of the Spirit such as tongues or prophecy. But the Greek word used is *laleo*, the ordinary word for 'speak'. If speaking in tongues were meant, some other word would have been used.
- It is about judging or weighing prophecy. However, there is nothing in the text to suggest that this would be a particular form of speech, and verse 35 makes it unlikely: the words more probably refer to some kind of informal talking or asking questions.
- Some interpreters have argued that the 'speaking' is teaching, and that this is what is forbidden. George Knight and others interpret verse 34 in the light of 1 Timothy 2, saying that Paul has already forbidden women's teaching, and that verse 34 agrees that women should not teach men. There are several problems with this view: verse 35 does not imply that sort of speaking, 1 Timothy 2 had not yet been written, and to interpret one difficult verse in terms of another gives an unreliable foundation for what has been built upon it.

Asking their husbands

Rejecting all of the above, Keener argues that 'speaking' most probably means asking questions in the service, and I find this the most consistent explanation. Questions were standard fare in ancient lecture settings, and women would have had less understanding of what was being taught. Paul encourages them to learn, but not in such a way as would be disruptive or socially inappropriate. The women, not understanding much of what was going on in the sermon, would have started talking among themselves or calling out and asking questions. It would have been inappropriate in their culture to ask other men in public. They should instead ask their husbands at home. None of this prohibits women today from speaking God's word.

A great deal of work has been done in the last few years on the cultural context of 1 Corinthians, which sheds more light on the situation that Paul was addressing. This last interpretation is favoured by Tom Wright, and makes sense, especially in the light of Paul's other concerns in the epistle for decency and order in worship.[20]

The idea of women asking their husbands at home *in order to help them learn* would have been one of the most challenging aspects of what Paul says, something that is usually lost on readers today. Greek and Roman culture deemed women to be inferior, and Jewish thought about women had strayed far from the egalitarian view found in Genesis 1 and 2, so men might well have assumed their wives incapable of engaging in theological discussion.

It is clear that these two passages in particular have been misread through most of the history of the Church, through the traditions we have inherited and the assumptions and cultural blinkers we have brought to the text. Far from putting a permanent bar on women's ministry, Paul promotes the idea of learning before speaking, which is applicable today to both men and women. The passages that have been held to be restrictive cannot be used in that way. If God calls them, women as well as men are called to serve in leadership at every level of the Church.

At the same time, the last few years have seen an increasing backlash against women's growing participation in church life. The concept of 'headship' has been refined, and some theologians have shifted the main arguments against women's leadership from these verses on to the idea of women's 'subordination', and on to the argument that God has always intended different 'roles' for men and women. This shift in goalposts also needs careful attention.

HEADSHIP, ROLE AND HIERARCHY

Written in 1987 by the founders of the Council on Biblical Manhood and Womanhood (an organization founded in the 1980s to counter the claims of biblical feminism), the Danvers Statement[21] sets out what it regards as appropriate roles for men and women, preserving male leadership in a way that it sees as scriptural. While the CBMW has most influence in America, it has some currency in Britain and other parts of the English-speaking world. It is probably the clearest comprehensive statement of what has become known as a 'complementarian' (more properly, 'hierarchical') view of the sexes, and includes the following points:

- Both Adam and Eve were created in God's image, equal before God as persons and distinct in their manhood and womanhood.
- Distinctions in masculine and feminine roles are ordained by God as part of the created order.
- Adam's headship in marriage was established by God before the Fall, and was not a result of sin.
- The Fall introduced distortions into the relationships between men and women. In the Church, sin inclines men toward a worldly love of power or an abdication of spiritual responsibility, and inclines women to resist limitations on their roles or to neglect the use of their gifts in appropriate ministries.
- Both Old and New Testaments also affirm the principle of male headship in the family and in the covenant community.
- Some governing and teaching roles within the Church are restricted to men.

Taking it at its most basic level, we may well ask what Genesis says about 'manhood' and 'womanhood', since those terms are very recent psychological constructs, as is the idea of 'role'. However, since these views have become widespread, and in some churches have led to women's leadership being restricted, we need to explore them in more detail.

The 'headship' issue

1 Corinthians 11:2–16 is another passage in Paul's letters that has long puzzled commentators. It is not clear what situation he is addressing, and several words and phrases are unclear, most notably the word 'head' (in Greek, *kephale*) in verse 3. But this verse, along with Ephesians 5:23, is the basis for the notion of 'headship' outlined above. While the latter verse has led to the teaching of hierarchy in marriage (the husband being 'head' of the wife and in the home), 1 Corinthians seems to have a wider reference and has been applied to the Church: 'the head of the woman is man' (NIV). This has been interpreted in a number of ways: a woman cannot be in overall leadership in the Church, since a man must always be 'head'; or, less commonly, a woman can lead if she is 'covered' or 'in submission' to a man. I have read of examples where, even at an all-women's church meeting, a man must be present so that the women who are leading have a 'head'.

A recent article by Alan Johnson in the journal *Priscilla Papers* helpfully sets out 50 years of debate over the word *kephale* in 1 Corinthians and Ephesians.[22] The two passages read (in the NIV) as follows:

1 Corinthians 11:3: 'But I want you to realize that the head of every man is Christ, and the head of the woman is man, and the head of Christ is God.'

Ephesians 5:23: 'For the husband is the head of the wife as Christ is the head of the church, his body, of which he is the Saviour.'

In the latter, Paul is more clearly talking about relationships in marriage; thus my discussion of 'headship' in relation to church leadership focuses mainly on 1 Corinthians.

How did the debate on the word 'head' unfold? Discussion of this passage goes back as long as biblical interpretation itself, but the starting point for the modern debate was an article in 1954 by Stephen Bedale. He sparked a storm by questioning the meaning of *kephale* as (figurative) 'head', and suggesting that it sometimes means 'first', 'beginning' or 'source'. Soon after, Morna Hooker added an important new insight to the interpretation of 1 Corinthians 11, that the word 'authority' in verse 10 refers not to a sign of male authority over a woman, but to the woman's own authority to participate fully in worship. In other words, head coverings are not a sign of subjection but a sign of women's authority.

James Hurley, writing in 1981, rejected the meaning 'source' for *kephale*. According to Hurley, 1 Corinthians establishes 'a hierarchy of headship authority' [God–Christ–man–woman]. In Ephesians, *kephale* has the same sense of 'head over' in relation to husbands and wives. Gilbert Bilezikian wrote *Beyond Sex Roles* (1985, and now in its third edition) principally to refute Hurley's thesis of male authority over women, arguing that *kephale* should in fact mean 'life-source, origin'.

Wayne Grudem wrote a couple of books that refuted the meaning 'source' as opposed to 'authority over', and set out as part of his argument the relationship between subordination and the Trinity— that from the time when the doctrine of the Trinity was established in AD325 it 'has been taken to imply a relationship between the Father and the Son that eternally existed and that will always exist—a relationship that includes a subordination in role, but not essence or being'.[23]

The discussion took an interesting turn with the publication of a book by Andrew Perriman. He argued that 1 Corinthians 11:3 must be understood as a metaphor, and that it has nothing to do with man's authority over a woman or any kind of hierarchy, but (as

Hooker suggested) was concerned with the shame that might come to a woman if she prayed or prophesied with her head uncovered. This was followed by a new slant from Judith Gundry-Volf (1997), who addressed the cultural context of the 1 Corinthians passage. Some of the believers in the church were ignoring social boundaries between men and women, signified by how they covered their heads. The women dishonoured the men (their 'heads') and men in turn shamed Christ (their 'head'). The meaning of the word *kephale* should be determined not from outside the passage but by looking at verses 3–5. Paul's words relate to a gender-based hierarchy in society that is no longer present; thus the verses do not apply to us in the same way as they did in Corinth.

Anthony Thiselton, in his 2000 commentary on 1 Corinthians, noted that arguing for *either* 'authority over' *or* 'source' as a clear meaning for *kephale* is hardly tenable any longer. However, Grudem wrote another response, concluding that 'authority over' as the meaning of *kephale* is 'firmly established', mainly on the basis of his earlier work, which examined 2336 examples of the word in ancient Greek literature and found none that meant 'source without authority'.[24] For Grudem it is crucial that *kephale* means 'person in authority over', giving unique authority to the husband in marriage and to men in the Church.

Beyond the debate on *kephale*

However, Grudem is substantially outweighed by others who conclude that the argument, as with other disputed texts, must be decided on contextual rather than purely lexical grounds. The word *kephale* should continue to be rendered 'head', yet without implying the freight that 'headship' brings to it. It seems clearer now, especially in the light of more awareness of the cultural background, that in 1 Corinthians 11 Paul was not talking about female insubordination to male authority. Instead, he wanted Christians to preserve cultural norms regarding visible gender distinctions for the sake of the mission of the Church. The issue was most probably that women had cast aside a cultural marker to do with their hairstyle, which distinguished them from men. Such a marker was significant only in the culture where such distinctions were needed; women's wearing of hats—one modern 'application' of this passage—does not have the same cultural significance. Paul's point is that while women *were* free in Christ, yet for the sake of the gospel they should conform to the norms of the time.

It is hard for us to think ourselves back into a culture of 2000 years ago, but a study of house churches in early Christianity, *A Woman's Place*,[25] enables us to do so in a fresh way. In writing to the Christians at Ephesus, Paul assumed a culture in which the man was head of the house, wives were frequently much younger, marriage was often impermanent and remarriage was common. In a context where wives were subject to their husbands (although they were the day-to-day managers of the household), much of Ephesians 5 would have sounded normal. What would have sounded unusual was the command to be subject to one another, the command to husbands to love their wives (sexual availability of slaves was taken for granted) and the picture of the Church as a bride, giving dignity to women who had little control over their bodies and destinies.

In other words, Paul introduced a new note of equality into a culture where relationships were strictly hierarchical. Today, when we no longer live according to such household codes, the abiding principle is mutual submission or natural deference. In Ephesians, Paul is talking about appropriate relations between husbands and wives (not all men and all women), which is not relevant to the subject of leadership in the Church.

Thus, however the word *kephale* should be understood in Ephesians 5, it applies within marriage rather than to all men and all women; and in 1 Corinthians the main point of the passage was conformity to the norms of the day. With understanding of *kephale* proving inconclusive, 'headship' cannot rest purely on this passage.

Women's leadership cannot be excluded on the basis of 1 Corinthians 11, but those who favour headship now look for support elsewhere.

Are women permanently subordinate?

In his book *Jesus and the Father: Modern Evangelicals Reinvent the Doctrine of the Trinity*,[26] Kevin Giles sets out to show how some conservative evangelicals have revived an old heretical view of the Trinity in order to support their view that women ought to be subordinated to men and thus ruled out of overall leadership in the Church. Male headship and female submission cannot be conclusively argued from the passages we have just explored, but an appeal to the Trinity moves the debate from a contentious verse to the doctrine of God and his intention for human beings from creation.

The view of 'role subordination', as it is known in its modern form, was first suggested in a book written in 1977 by George Knight III, *The New Testament Teaching on the Role Relationship of Men and Women*, in response to growing concern among some evangelicals about the role of women in the Church. Knight argued that women were not subordinate to men in being, nature or essence, but rather in role, function and authority. Thus he rejected popular ideas of women's inferiority which stemmed from antiquity and persisted until the early 20th century, but proposed in its place a new justification of inequality in role and function: 'just as woman is created equal to man but has a subordinate role at home and in church, so the Son of God is coequal with the Father in being or essence but has a subordinate role in the work of salvation and in all eternity'.[27] This teaching was taken up by Wayne Grudem, who has been one of its chief proponents.

Grudem and others make no apology for arguing 'role subordination' as a way of keeping women out of many areas of ministry. Women's 'role' is subordinate to men's—permanently—and this permanent subordination is anchored in the permanent subordination of 'roles' within God himself. What is perhaps most surprising,

41

especially to the critics of role subordination, is that they claim that this view of the Trinity is the historic one.

Subordination in the Trinity?

The doctrine of the Trinity is not found explicitly in the Bible but arose in the early Church as a response to various forms of heretical teaching about Jesus. In essence it asserts that Jesus is truly God— just as truly God as God the Father, even though he is different from the Father. The Council of Nicaea, held in AD325, rejected a subordinationist heresy known as Arianism, and ruled out every form of subordination in the Godhead.

There are verses in scripture where Jesus appears to put the Father above him—'the Father is greater than I', for example (John 14:28)— but human obedience is not the same as divine being. 'Subordination' is not biblical terminology; Christ humbled himself in a way much better described as self-humiliation rather than subordination. It is clear in scripture that Jesus is fully God: 'I and the Father are one' (John 10:30).

Another argument for subordination is to propose that because Jesus seems to have existed *after* the Father, he must be regarded as a creation. This is the essence of Arianism—that Jesus is the first and highest thing that God made, but not fully God. Hence the phrase in the Nicene Creed, which many Anglicans say in worship each week, that Jesus is 'begotten not made'. I was teaching the history of the creeds to a group of trainee lay ministers recently, and most of them did not feel that the details of whether Jesus was *homoousios* ('of the same substance') or *homoiousios* ('of a similar substance') were very relevant to their lives and ministries. But in this context they are crucial. The Son and the Father share the same substance or being; the divine being of Jesus is no different from the divine being of the Father.

Beyond Nicaea

Battles around this concept continued for some time after Nicaea. In order to clarify the way in which God works, the ancient theologians came to express it as an 'order' in which the persons of the Trinity operate. For example, the work of salvation is initiated by the Father, who sent the Son; and the Spirit works to convict people of their sin, turn them towards Christ and perfect the body of Christ for eternal life. This difference in 'order' is not the same as a difference in 'roles', however. There is only one divine will, not three wills (like three people agreeing to work together). There cannot, then, be positions of authority and subordination, because that implies more than one will. Nicaean orthodoxy says that there is only one will in God; the Son's is not different from the Father's, so there can be no parallel distinction of man and woman.

In addition, the logic of 1 Corinthians 11:3 works against this hierarchical interpretation. The text does not say, 'Now I want you to know that God is the head of Christ, and Christ is the head of man, and man is the head of woman.' Paul lists Christ first and God last. It makes more sense to see this as an order of chronology: Christ is the fountainhead of every man, man the source of a woman, God is the fountainhead of Christ.[28]

Thus, for a whole host of reasons, the idea of 'role subordination' based on the Trinity is untenable. Sadly, however, the view has caught on in a wide range of evangelical circles. It sounds convincing: 'men and women are equal; they have simply been given different and complementary roles.' We often think there *are* clear differences between the sexes—that, in the popular view, 'men are from Mars and women are from Venus'. It seems to make sense to find this in scripture, that God intended it from the beginning. The final plank in this argument is that scriptural proof for the view is found in 1 Timothy 2:11–14, the often quoted passage which was supposed to settle everything. The choice is clear: accept the Bible's teaching, or not!

If 1 Timothy does not suggest that women should not teach, however, then one piece of this argument is removed, and it becomes circular. Mainstream theologians on the doctrine of the Trinity do not support it. The 'role subordination' view of the Trinity is certainly neither as historical nor as traditional as is claimed.

What about 'role'?

Suspicions about 'role subordination' may be aroused by the use of the word 'role'. The word 'role' is never used in theological texts and biblical commentaries before 1970;[29] it is a relatively modern term, drawn originally from the theatre but used in sociology from the 1930s, and more widely from the 1960s. There is nowhere in the Bible where fixed roles are prescribed on the basis of gender. The idea that the Bible defines 'masculinity' and 'femininity' is ludicrous when we bear in mind that these terms are modern constructs to describe sets of gender stereotypes. God does not give gifts in two versions, pink and blue. God calls people, he equips them with gifts, but our basic identity before God is not in what we do but in who we are.

Games in Genesis

Related novelties have also crept into interpretations of Genesis:[30]

- that the chronological order in which the man and woman were created implies a binding social order that gives priority to men.
- that Adam was invested with the position of leadership, authority and responsibility to keep the garden before Eve was created.
- that God prepared Adam for his leadership role by having him name the living creatures.[31]
- that Adam needed a 'helper': 'Up to this point Adam's helper/companion had been God; now God supplied him with a human helper who would not threaten him by being superior or equal

in physical strength, but a perfectly formed "weaker vessel" who would respond to his love and his need for companionship.'[32]

• that Eve should have deferred to her 'head' Adam rather than taking the 'lead' in eating the fruit.

These arguments have been well answered in much more detail elsewhere,[33] but they continue to appear, so a brief discussion follows here of two of them: creation order, and the significance of the word *ezer*.

Order in creation

While at theological college in the early 1990s, I found myself leading a seminar with the title 'The crisis in relations between the sexes in our society is due to its rejection of the differentiated relations between men and women found in the Old Testament'. I produced a short introductory paper, starting with the following rather provocative words: 'This is clearly ridiculous. If there is a crisis in relations between the sexes in our society it is because at last women have become fed up with being doormats, and those who find themselves giving up power seldom like it.'

I went on to discuss briefly Genesis 2 and 3, and the suggestion made by some that there is significance in the priority of creation. If there is significance in the priority of creation, I have always liked the idea that God made Adam first (after the rest of creation, of course) and that when he had finished, he looked at Adam and said to himself, 'Well, I think I could do better than that if I tried again.'

I would not propose that as a serious argument; however, the order of creation cannot itself be held to imply priority. If it were, animals might well be the leaders of human beings, since they were created before us. In Genesis 1, the emphasis is on equality: God created human beings in his image, male and female (v. 27). In Genesis 2, Adam's response to Eve is that she is like him (v. 23), not that she is his subordinate. It is commonality rather than complementarity. The creation of Eve was not intended to show a creation order of power, but to reveal unity of flesh and purpose. What went wrong at the Fall was the entry of overbearing authority and domination into a world intended for partnership. And ever since, history has been a battle between the pattern of mutual submission and servanthood and that of domination and rulership.

Does ezer imply a male/female priority?

The Hebrew word *ezer* ('helper'), used of Eve in Genesis 2:18, is sometimes held to imply her inferiority, but the same word is also used of God himself in Genesis 49:25. The context suggests what kind of 'help' is needed, and whether the helper should be considered an inferior or superior or equal. At this point, the man needs help to alleviate his aloneness. He needs a friend, a partner, and he cannot find one in the animal kingdom. In addition (as I mentioned above), when he meets the woman, he cries, 'This is now bone of my bones and flesh of my flesh' (Genesis 2:23). The emphasis is on sameness, not difference: 'here is one like me!'

Another significant verse in establishing what God intended for men and women is Genesis 2:24: 'a man will leave his father and mother and be united to his wife, and they will become one flesh'. I can still remember from some years ago the pain of a young Bangladeshi colleague who discovered that she had married 'into' her husband's family and was more or less a prisoner in that home. I can remember thanking God for this verse, suggesting an equality in marriage that was remarkably radical in its time, and for the way in which God has designed it so that a woman who marries is less likely to become her husband's subordinate.

Each of the arguments from Genesis that have been used to imply a creation order of men and women is thus capable of a very different interpretation. This discussion of role subordination is necessarily brief, and the Resources Section at the end of this book includes titles that discuss the issue in far greater detail.

Women and slaves

Those who argue for subordination have also been the first to make a distinction between advice given to women and advice to slaves where they stand side by side in scripture (for example, in Colossians 3:18–22 and 4:1)—suggesting that the former is permanent and the latter is not. Again, this does not stand up to historical scrutiny. If it were true, slavery would have been abolished long ago. But 250 years ago many Western Christians argued from the Bible that slavery was ordained by God. Fundamental to the abolitionist argument, on the other hand, was an attempt to move beyond the specific wording of the text, which could be held to support slavery, and instead to appeal to its spirit and the wider culture.

The attitude of Jesus and Paul to the social customs of their day was often ambiguous, and, if we wonder why God allowed slavery to persist for so long, we have to conclude that in such matters God accommodates himself to human limitations. The majority of American Christians before the Civil War thought it impossible to condemn slavery on biblical grounds. But when biblical arguments for its abolition were put alongside the demolishing of cultural assumptions about race, the resulting biblical and theological principles implied that slavery was evil and should be abolished. No Christian would defend it now.

Many Christians today argue that patriarchy was the inevitable theological result of the biblical Fall—but, like slavery, was so deeply embedded in the cultures of Old and New Testament times that, despite its critique by Jesus and Paul, the time was not right for its abolition.[34] Similar assumptions lay behind the existence of slavery and of patriarchy—about superiority (of white over non-white, men over women) and privilege (the Fall has meant that our judgments and perceptions may always be clouded by self-interest). Nevertheless, the seeds of a complementary rather than hierarchical relation between the sexes were implicit from creation, and have been perceived throughout the centuries by many Christians. It is only tragic that at the present time, when women have at last proved that they are the equal of men in their abilities, they should find the Church denying them the opportunity to use those abilities.

Finally in this section, having explored a variety of arguments used by evangelicals, we will briefly consider some of the arguments from the Catholic wing of the Church.

ARGUMENTS FROM TRADITION

The book *Consecrated Women?*[35] written as a contribution to the debate about women bishops, provides a useful guide to issues about women in leadership on the Catholic wing of the Church. These include the fact that there were no women apostles, priests or bishops in the early Church; the maleness of Jesus Christ, which means that a woman cannot represent Christ and so cannot be a priest; as well as issues of scripture, headship and difference in role, already discussed above.

Women leaders in the early Church?

As the following chapter shows, there is much more historical precedent for women in leadership roles than many Christians seem to realize, both in scripture (evident in the book of Acts and various epistles) and in the first 600 years of church history. However, we should note that it is impossible to establish arguments from precedent in relation to particular roles or offices. This is partly because it is far from clear that the three 'offices' of bishop, priest and deacon, which emerged in the later New Testament period, were distinct from one another, let alone how those offices of nearly 2000 years ago relate to our situation today. What is clear is that women did hold a variety of ministry and leadership roles in the early Church.

Who can represent Christ?

Christ was incarnated as a male person: that much cannot be disputed. However, sometimes too much is made of Christ's maleness. Stress on the Fatherhood of God can imply that God is 'male' rather than beyond gender. Assumptions are made about the significance of Christ's maleness as redeemer, while Philippians 2 tells us that Jesus took *human* form and *human* likeness—in other words, stressing his humanity, not his maleness. This is another case where accurate translation of the Greek is essential for our correct understanding.

It is argued that the Jewish priesthood was restricted to men for theological reasons—in contradiction to the pagan shrines served by priestesses—and that only a male priesthood could represent the whole community before God.[36] What was valid in one unique situation, however, does not have to dictate what should be valid in a different historical context. To build on Christ's maleness the assumption that a woman cannot preside at the Eucharist goes beyond logical argument, placing on maleness a privilege that scripture never gives it. Jesus' maleness may have been compelling, may have told people something about God, within a patriarchal culture, but it does so no longer.[37]

This view is connected in some church traditions to typology: the priest is in the place of Christ, and women cannot represent Christ. But this use of typology has been challenged. While typology is about Christ being prefigured by Melchizedek, the blood of the lambs at the exodus, or Jonah, for example, to use it in relation to women and the priesthood is to use this approach back to front. A different way of looking at the issue would be to see that a woman can represent humanity in her response to Christ: the Catholic and Eastern traditions might well look to Mary, a type of every believer in her response to God. By this approach to typology, the priesthood of the Church could properly be represented by either a man or a woman.[38]

What God longs for is that those whom he calls and gifts should minister, building up the body of Christ and equipping others. Women and men are indeed called to lead—and called to lead not in opposition to one another, as if only one gender can have 'power', but alongside one another, together reflecting the image of God and bringing the fullest range of gifts and talents to serve God. As Lorry Lutz concludes in her book *Women as Risk-takers for God*, 'When the "middle wall of partition" is broken down between men and women, the synergism of male–female partnership may well be the greatest redemptive force this world has seen since Pentecost.'[39]

QUESTIONS FOR REFLECTION AND DISCUSSION

- What scriptural arguments have you heard that bar women from leadership? Do you find them convincing? How can you address them?
- Why does the Bible translation we use make a difference to how we interpret scripture?
- If a woman who feels called to leadership finds herself in a church where she is not allowed to exercise her calling, what should she do? Stay and be quiet? Stay and challenge? Is the debate a public one or a private one?

✧

Chapter 2

LEADING WOMEN

'One of the best-kept secrets in Christianity is the enormous role that women played in the early church.'
CATHERINE C. KROEGER

'What women these Christians have!'
LIBIANUS, FOURTH-CENTURY PAGAN PHILOSOPHER

We can hardly discuss the biblical case for leadership without looking at women leaders in scripture, but the mere presence of women there does not decide the question of women in leadership today. It is important to consider whether the women in scripture were 'exceptions that prove the rule' (that men should lead) or whether they were people whom God used to further his kingdom, their fewness being more a reflection of society at that time than of God's design.

If God intended men and women to share together as equals in the care of his creation and the leadership of his Church, then we would expect to see examples in scripture. At the same time, in the patriarchal world of the Old Testament and of Jesus' day, we would not expect to see many women emerging as leaders.

In fact, we certainly do see a number of women leaders in both Old and New Testaments. In the Old Testament, a few women are gifted for particular tasks. The presence of women leaders is unusual but not treated as such—and in the New Testament there is a sign that God, having poured out his Spirit on both men and women, calls and equips both for leadership in his new community, the Church.

We still live in the 'between times'; God's kingdom has not fully come. The women whose stories are briefly explored in this chapter are the 'firstfruits' of the egalitarian trajectory, intended from creation, which is opened up in the new covenant.

THE OLD TESTAMENT

It is important to read the Old Testament with an awareness that its culture—or cultures—were very different from those of Western society today. Society was hierarchical and patriarchal; this was taken for granted. The father was the legal head of the household and every woman was under the authority of some man, first her father, then her husband. Sometimes it seems that women were almost seen as chattels—in the Ten Commandments, for example, where 'your neighbour's wife' is among a list of his possessions not to be coveted (Exodus 20:17). Only a few verses earlier, however, equal honour is to be shown to both fathers and mothers (v. 12). Then again, a woman could not divorce her husband, and daughters and wives could not inherit property from their father or husband. The case in Numbers 27:1–11 where the daughters of Zelophehad asked, and were allowed, to inherit their father's property is clearly a change to an existing norm.

But while the male was the leader of the household, personality, then as now, was a factor in human behaviour and relationships. There are examples of husbands who loved their wives deeply and treated them as equals—Elkanah and Hannah, for example (1 Samuel 1). Daughters shared in family life as much as sons, both participated in religious festivals, and a number of women took on a variety of leadership roles.

Miriam

The main way in which women were able to exercise leadership in the Old Testament was in the role of prophet. The prophet's role was to listen to God and speak as his voice to the people, to reveal God's will and challenge the people to follow him and be faithful to him, warning of the consequences if they did not. While prophets are popularly thought of as 'foretelling', the role of biblical prophets was more to do with 'forth-telling'.

Miriam, Moses' elder sister, was honoured in the eighth century BC by the prophet Micah, who bracketed her with Aaron and Moses as Israel's 'leaders', even though at one point she had turned against Moses. It was Miriam whose clever idea enabled her infant brother both to live and to be reared by his own mother when neither seemed possible, and the song in Exodus 15 is ascribed to Moses and Miriam, which suggests, with the Micah reference, that she shared in leadership with Moses and Aaron. In Exodus 15:20 she is clearly seen as a prophet, and leader of the women, reminding her people of the power and importance of celebration.

Deborah, prophet and judge

Deborah was both a prophet and a judge. Her story is told in two forms: in narrative form in Judges 4 and in poetic form in the following chapter. In the light of Miriam's song, this is itself worth noting: accounts of these two women are given in both linear and poetic styles, giving increased emphasis to their presence.

The verb 'to judge' used of Deborah is the same word that is used 20 times in the book of Judges and elsewhere for those who delivered Israel from their enemies. She was clearly the leader of God's people at that time. She held court under the Palm of Deborah (Judges 4:5); people went to her for wisdom in settling their disputes, and there is no mistaking the authoritative tone in her words and actions. At a time of danger for Israel, she provided guidance, encouragement and ultimately thanksgiving for a great military victory over the enemy.

Deborah needed someone to lead the army and we see her summon and appoint Barak. He was not immediately convinced about her battle plan and responded, 'If you go with me, I will go; but if you don't go with me, I won't go' (4:8). It seems most likely that, as she was the leader and she had heard from God, Barak did not want to venture out without her presence.

At any rate, Deborah listened to Barak and agreed to accompany him. Thus they demonstrated partnership in leading—Deborah bringing spiritual power and Barak military might. Together they were able to free God's people from occupying forces. Deborah was another leader who knew the power of praise, and under her collaborative leadership the people of the region lived in peace for 40 years. The fact that she was a woman leader is not commented on in the text.

The prophet Huldah

When the famous Book of the Law was found in the temple in Jerusalem, which of the prophets did Josiah's advisers consult? There were a number that they could have consulted, but they chose Huldah: 'Hilkiah and those the king had sent with him went to speak to the prophet Huldah, who was the wife of Shallum... She lived in Jerusalem, in the New Quarter' (2 Chronicles 34:22)

Huldah did not defer to any male leadership but accepted the responsibility of hearing from God. She gave the advisers a message to take to the king and he acted on it. He did not check it out with a male prophet to see if Huldah was correct. As with Deborah, there is no sign that she was seen as exceptional, no comment on the fact that she was a woman.

Women served as prophets—spokespersons for God—at some key junctures in Israel's history, and it is worth noting that women were not simply used at times when there were no suitable male leaders, as is sometimes argued. Miriam, Deborah and Huldah ministered in the context of significant male leaders.

'For such a time as this'

Esther lived long after the era of the exodus and the judges, in the Persian capital of Susa, during the reign of Xerxes. While she had no formal leadership role—she was not a prophet or a judge—her story shows that women could exercise leadership in a range of ways and that, in being open to God, an obedient woman could be used in a remarkable way.

Esther was an Israelite, taken captive by the Persian king and eventually made his queen. In the midst of the splendour in which she found herself, Esther learned that her people were threatened with extinction by a law engineered by a close associate of the king. She realized that she was uniquely placed to act and counter the king, in order to alter the course of events and save the Jews. As her uncle Mordecai urged her to act, he spoke words that have resonated with many leaders challenged to take courage and step up to a new level of authority: 'And who knows but that you have come to royal position for such a time as this?' (Esther 4:14). Her prayer, godly wisdom and diplomacy make her a good role model for leaders of both sexes.

The book ends with a record of how the feast of Purim was established, 'the time when the Jews got relief from their enemies, and... the month when their sorrow was turned into joy' (9:22). It was through Esther's leadership that the people were brought to a time of rejoicing.

In addition to those above, we can also count as Old Testament women leaders the Shunammite woman (2 Kings 4), Abigail (1 Samuel 25) and at times Sarah (Genesis 21:12). There may have been only a few female prophets, and women were not eligible for the priesthood (nor were men who were not descendants of Aaron). There is no indication within the Old Testament that women were ineligible for or incapable of leadership or authority. As Mary Evans concludes, 'that women leaders did exist in a society where women were considered inferior is significant'.[1]

THE NEW TESTAMENT

Women leaders become more prominent as the Church comes into being. The biblical affirmation of women as prophets continues into the Gospels with Anna (Luke 2:36–38); and after Pentecost, when the Spirit was poured out on all believers, we see women and men prophesying as part of worship (1 Corinthians 11:4–5).

There are signs in the Gospels of what was to come: examples of Jesus' dealings with women are well known, but it is worth looking again at the accounts of the woman at the well, and the fact that women were last at the cross and first at the tomb. Yes, Jesus chose twelve male apostles, but there were all kinds of reasons why this would be so in the religious and cultural world of that time, and Jesus' choice of twelve close associates also symbolized his plan to renew God's people, Israel.[2]

Mary Magdalene was an outstanding disciple, which partly accounts for the fascination with her story through the last 2000 years. It was to her, rather than to any of the men, that Jesus entrusted the good news of the resurrection. Mary qualifies as an apostle if an apostle was one who followed Jesus and personally witnessed the resurrection, and she has been described as the 'apostle to the apostles'.[3] She also appears to have been a leader among the women. In fact, Luke highlights Mary, Joanna and Susanna among the women, just as Peter, James and John are often the focus among the Twelve.

Being with Jesus

A passage in the Gospels that is often overlooked is Luke 8:1–3, the first time in that Gospel when we are introduced to the idea that among Jesus' travelling companions was a body of women. If the choosing of the Twelve in Mark's Gospel (3:13–19) is compared to the account in Luke (6:12–16), it is worth noting that Luke's version omits some of Mark's points in order to use them here. Luke 8:1–2 tells us that the Twelve were 'with him, and also some women', which suggests that there is some parity between the two groups in being 'with him'—in other words, accompanying him as disciples. Secondly, they are sent out to preach, following Jesus' example, as we see more explicitly for the Twelve (9:1) and the seventy-two (10:1–24). Luke also looks ahead; whereas Mark does not let us know that women were travelling with Jesus until his account of the crucifixion (Mark 15:40–41), Luke makes it clear here, so that we keep the women in mind for the rest of the story.

It would be too much to say that the women are a parallel body of apostles, but Luke is moving in that direction. For Luke, these women have an importance that parallels the importance of the Twelve.[4] This means that if we use Mark 3 to speak of how Jesus developed leaders, it is quite legitimate to include women among them.

Furthermore, the way that Luke again and again sets women and men in parallel (for example, Zechariah and Mary in chapter 1; the centurion and the widow in chapter 7; stories of a lost sheep and a lost coin in Luke 15) suggests that something very significant is happening. Luke has not written women out of the beginning of Christianity, as some have argued, but written them in. Women and men have equal importance and value before God.

It is also worth pausing to consider Mary of Bethany in Luke 10:38–42. This passage has been much interpreted and is often used to contrast the busy Martha with the contemplative Mary. But in the context of women's leadership the passage is much more significant. It would have been obvious to contemporary readers, first, that Mary was sitting at Jesus' feet in the male part of the house rather than in the back rooms with the women, and second, that 'sitting at his feet' was meant to signify that Mary was a student, picking up Jesus' teaching—in order that one day she would herself be a teacher and leader. Tom Wright comments, 'Examples like Mary's, no doubt, are at least part of the reason why we find so many women in positions of leadership, responsibility and initiative in the early church.'[5]

Both men and women

At Pentecost the Spirit was poured out in fulfilment of Joel's prophecy, which Peter quotes in explanation:

In the last days, God says, I will pour out my Spirit on all people. Your sons and daughters will prophesy, your young men will see visions, your old men will dream dreams. Even on my servants, both men and women, I will pour out my Spirit in those days, and they will prophesy. (Acts 2:17–18)

Many have looked to these verses in seeking to make sense of Bible passages that seemed to prohibit women's public ministry. Despite their small numbers, it was always God's intention that men and women should work side by side in prophetic ministry and in leadership, as did Miriam with Moses and Aaron, Deborah with Barak, and Huldah with Jeremiah and others. But here it is made much clearer: ministry is for all on whom God pours his Spirit and gifts as he wills; gender is irrelevant.

As we look at the early Church, another point which is often missed is that, when persecution takes place, women are targeted alongside men (Acts 8:3). Tom Wright cites Ken Bailey's insight that 'this only makes sense if the women, too, are seen as leaders and influential figures within the community'.[6]

'Our sister Phoebe'

Romans 16 is an important chapter, although at first sight it appears to be little worthy of attention, being mainly a list of names of those whom Paul wishes to greet. But there are a number of women's names here, and they are significant.

First comes Phoebe, a woman whose role has been much disputed. Paul's (Greek) word for her church position is *diakonos*; this is the first reference to a woman as 'deacon', but precisely what this role entailed is unclear. What is fascinating, however, is that in some translations Phoebe is described here as a 'servant', while when Paul uses the same word of himself and others it is translated 'deacon' or 'minister'. There is now a general trend, both in translations and commentaries, towards recognizing Phoebe as a church leader, after centuries of relegating her to a 'servant' role.

Phoebe is also referred to as *prostatis* (v. 2), translated as 'helper' in the RSV and 'a great help' in NIV. This Greek word means 'patron', and recent research enables us to understand more about what it entailed. Underlying the earliest Christian communities was a complex model of social networks based on informal and asymmetrical relationships for the exchange of goods and resources, creating relationships of patrons and recipients. Women were patrons in the same way as men, and their patronage of churches is key.

Thus, while it has often been assumed that Phoebe as *prostatis* was an inferior, when we understand the patronage system we can see that it is 'the one who received who had to recognize subordination'.[7] Paul is thus in Phoebe's debt—which may be one of a number of reasons why she is mentioned first in this chapter. He had relied on her to pave the way in Rome for him, and she was possibly involved in his plans for mission to Spain. A notable leader, generous benefactor and model disciple, indeed!

'Outstanding among the apostles'

Much ink has been spilt over the name Junia, whom Paul describes as 'prominent among the apostles' (Romans 16:7). What has been at stake is the question of how the Greek name *Iounian* should be translated. Is it Junia? Or is it Junias, making the person a man?

Junia has, in fact, long been recognized as a woman; Chrysostom writes, 'Oh! How great is the devotion of this woman, that she should be even counted worthy of the appellation of apostle', and the name is given as Junia in the King James Bible. It is increasingly clear that there are no historical or exegetical arguments for thinking the name to be a male form.[8] The name 'Junias' is unknown in any records, while 'Junia' was common. Some commentators seem to have assumed that women cannot be apostles, so Junia the apostle must be a man, but this has been shown to be quite unwarranted reasoning. The word 'apostle' is used to refer to those who had seen the resurrected Christ, which could apply to her; and Paul uses it more widely still, to mean something like 'church planter'. This could also cover Junia, who was most probably part of a husband-and-wife church planting team with her husband Andronicus.

Considerable scholarly work has been done on this chapter recently, proving that it is a far from unimportant list. Those named and commended were leaders of the Roman house churches, congregations that did not have the leisure to debate whether or not women could lead but acted as the Spirit led.

A woman's place

The study by Osiek and Macdonald on the role of women in the house churches (up to the middle of the second century) concludes that 'women participated in all the activities of the house church in the first generation of the Christian era and that the house church was the centre for worship, hospitality, patronage, education, communications, social services, evangelization and mission'.[9] In house churches where the household leader was a woman, she would probably have hosted formal dinners and presided at them, including the assembly of the 'church'. Examples of these hostesses are the mother of John Mark (Acts 12:12–17), Lydia (16:40) and Nympha (Colossians 4:15). Others may have included Phoebe, and Euodia and Syntyche.

The hostess led the blessing and sharing of the bread and cup during the meal. There was no particular anxiety about qualifications of leaders in ritual meals at this stage. Teaching, however, was different, and a trained person was required. Education would have happened in homes, some in mixed groups but much in same-sex groups (for cultural, not theological, reasons). Resistance to women in positions of authority in mixed assembly gradually increased due to traditional norms that sought to silence women in public functions, and perhaps also because of heretical movements like the Montanists, where women were given a fuller role. The functions of presiding at the meal and teaching were separate at this time, but came together during the second century when the model of the teaching presbyter bishop arose.[10]

Recent studies on the Philippian church have concluded that female believers played prominent roles in the development of the congregation. The first convert was Lydia, and the church first met in her house (Acts 16:40), while Euodia and Syntyche were leaders (Philippians 4:2–3). Their dispute was not about the flower rota, as a friend reported that he had heard preached from a pulpit recently. If their disagreement had been on that level, would Paul really have bothered to write about it? Paul here, as in many of the letters, is writing about conflict; as leaders, the women's disagreement jeopardized the unity and mission of the church.

Partnership in mission

Priscilla, named six times in the book of Acts, was part of another husband-and-wife leadership duo. She and Aquila are twice greeted as co-workers, and the language Paul uses suggests that they had a church planting ministry similar to his own. They seem to have been both itinerant ministers (we can track their journeys from Rome to Corinth to Ephesus and back to Rome) and leaders of house churches, including one that met in their home in Rome (Romans 16:5).[11] In Roman culture, as in our own, a man's name would normally appear first when speaking of a couple, but the fact that Priscilla is named first four out of six times suggests that she was the more prominent leader.

More briefly, Philip's four daughters were prophets at Caesarea (Acts 21:9), and Nympha was responsible for the church that met in her house (Colossians 4:15).

It is important to put these scripture references to women in leadership alongside the small number of debated passages discussed in the last chapter. The Bible shows that some women were leaders, occasionally in the Old Testament and more significantly after Pentecost. While we see fewer women leaders than men in the New Testament Church, there is no indication of a hierarchy in leadership between men and women. By showing a new attitude to women and singling out some for future leadership, Jesus began to change the paradigm; Paul followed, in his practice and in his writings. There are particular reasons why women then disappeared from leadership after a couple of centuries, but there is every reason why, as a church that longs to be true to scripture, we should affirm godly women as leaders at every level in the Church.

THE PATRISTIC PERIOD

The debate in various churches over women's ordination as priests or pastors has sparked a number of studies of women in the early Church over the past 30 years. Were women 'ordained' and, if so, to what ministries? While we have access to various apostolic teachings of the third to fifth centuries, evidence is still coming to light about the kinds of leadership that women exercised, and their implications for women's leadership today.

Documents of the Church

The time from around AD100 to the Council of Chalcedon in 451 is known as the patristic period. At this time, many questions of doctrine and practice arose, which were debated in councils and written about in various documents by those who came to be known as the Church Fathers (hence the name 'patristic', from Latin *pater,* 'father'). The debate about women's leadership can be traced through some of these documents, as well as more implicitly tracked through literary texts and allusions, and inscriptions. The book *Ordained Women in the Early Church*[12] records every piece of known evidence for women deacons and priests, at least in the Greek- and Latin-speaking worlds, up to AD600. The authors helpfully distinguish between the Eastern and Western churches, where patterns of ministry emerged differently.

The *Apostolic Tradition,* written by Hippolytus in the early third century, reveals the beginning of moves towards more fixed offices and a specific rite of ordination, and says that widows were not to be ordained. The *Didascalia Apostolorum*, also dating from the third century and written in Syria, reflects further controversy, and places further restrictions on widows: they were not to preach and teach or visit homes to instruct believers, which seems to reflect the need for women to conform to gender expectations in that society. It is the earliest church text to describe the office of female deacons.

The *Apostolic Constitutions*, a compilation of church orders including the *Didascalia*, dates from the late fourth century. This contains the words used at the 'ordination of the deaconess'.[13] References to Miriam, Sarah, Anna and Huldah show how deaconesses were seen as serving in the line of biblical prophetesses, and the prayer also invokes the Holy Spirit. However, expressions in the prayers such as 'cleanse her from all filthiness of flesh and spirit' reveal how concerns about female uncleanness affected views of women's ministry.

The Council of Chalcedon set down requirements for the ordination of deaconesses. The titles *diakonos* and *diakonissa* existed side by side for some time after the fourth century. At first there was no distinction, but by the third century a special office of female deacon or deaconess had developed in the East, intended especially for ministry to women. For example, women needed to be involved in the baptism of women by immersion, and in visiting women in their homes, which would have been regarded as improper for male deacons. In some other contexts their roles overlapped with male deacons. The institution of female deacons did not arise in the West until the fifth century, and much about them remains unknown.

The Council of Laodicea (probably the one in the late fourth or early fifth century) disbanded the office of presbyteress (from which we can assume that it existed up to this point): 'Concerning those who are called presbytides or female presiders (*prokathemenai*), it is not permitted to appoint them in the Church' (Council of Laodicea, Canon 11).[14] The word 'presider' here means a female who takes the front seat or the position of leader or presider in worship. The title 'presbyter', in its masculine and feminine forms, is always subject to interpretation according to context. Both can mean an elderly person or an office-holder (a presbyter), and in the feminine form it can also mean the wife of a male presbyter. Synods and councils of the West and East condemned the practice of women presbyters—which makes it clear that they existed, even if in small numbers.

Madigan and Osiek conclude their study: 'What can be said with certainty is that the claim that women have never functioned as presbyters in the "orthodox" church is simply untrue.'[15]

'It is not permitted'

So why did women disappear from leadership during these years? In Christian writers of the first to second centuries, there is little suggestion that women's ministry was controversial, possibly because leadership was less fixed and depended on charism rather than office.

But there are a number of reasons why women ceased to exercise leadership roles from around the sixth century

Various answers are suggested by historians. One is that it was a reaction against heresies, in which women definitely did take a lead. The Montanists had women as both bishops and presbyters, and anti-Montanist literature focused on the leadership of women. Marcion is said to have appointed women to all church offices on an equal basis with men, and Gnostic groups also attracted women. Many writers in the early Church believed that women were more vulnerable to error and therefore could not be trusted as leaders. Sadly, this argument is still advanced occasionally today.[16]

A reason advanced by Madigan and Osiek[17] is the rise of 'cultic sacramentalism', which highlighted purity for those who would lead the Eucharist. Cultic purity was associated with males, impurity with females, because of the blood of menstruation and childbirth. This was the biggest argument against women presbyters. (Celibacy was a requirement for men, though often ignored.)

Another reason is the custom of baptism by full immersion, which required nudity and the anointing of the entire body by the baptizing clergy. Thus women clergy were required to baptize female converts—but when infant baptism became the norm, female clergy were no longer needed.

It is also suggested that a key reason was the gradual shift of the Church, around the third century, from the private sphere (meeting in homes) to the public. At the same time, the threefold order of ministry began to emerge, and women were increasingly excluded from these fixed offices. As leadership became formalized, it became less gift-based and more tied to position, a pattern repeated many times in church history as the freedom to lead and minister was tied down by rules and regulations about who could do what. In addition, the pressure of conforming to a patriarchal culture militated against the young Church taking such a radically countercultural step as having women in its leadership. What might seem normal to us was off the radar for most people of that era.

Any of these reasons could have been revisited later as customs changed—yet it has taken 1400 years. If the main reasons for excluding women from leadership positions in the early Church were cultural rather than scriptural, there is no need any longer to maintain this exclusion.

QUESTIONS FOR REFLECTION AND DISCUSSION

- How do you think the examples of women leaders in scripture should inform the debate about leadership today?
- Why do you think we hear so little about women leaders in scripture and the early Church? What can you do in your own circles to change this?

Chapter 3

TELLING STORIES

'To follow the voice of the Church apart from that of the written Word has never proved safe; but, on the other hand, it may be that we need to be admonished not to ignore the teaching of the deepest spiritual life of the Church in forming our conclusions concerning the meaning of Scripture. It cannot be denied that in every great spiritual awakening in the history of Protestantism the impulse for Christian women to pray and witness for Christ in the public assembly has been found irrepressible.'[1]

It is sometimes argued that women should not be leaders in the Church today because we have not had women leaders through 2000 years of church history. We have already seen how mistaken that view is, with regard to the early Church. It is also mistaken in relation to more recent history. Women may have been excluded from most formal leadership positions, but in every age women have led.

Yet so many people, men and women, do not know those stories, stories of women who have been leaders despite the barriers they often faced. Young Sawa Kim, an ordained Korean pastor who was serving in Japan in the 1980s, decided that for this reason she must write her autobiography: 'I came to know what feminists say when they say, "History = His Story". If I would not write my story (Her Story), even my daughters would not know how their mother lived or thought.'

One way in which women have sought to empower themselves, and correct the imbalances of the history they have received, is to recapture the stories of women of history. The purpose of this chapter is to recover something of 'herstory' and uncover just a few of the remarkable examples of women who have answered God's call to leadership.

THE EARLY CHURCH

Despite the fact that women were excluded from most areas of church leadership after the first few centuries, there have always been exceptions—women who have been able to transcend their culture and take on leadership roles. Notable leaders who helped to shape the early Church included Marcella, Paula and Macrina.

Marcella

Born into a noble Roman family in 325, Marcella was widowed at an early age and, rather than marry again, devoted herself to serving God. She was one of the first people to form a monastic community in Rome; here, she and others studied the Bible in Greek and Hebrew. She was sought out for debate and discussion of scripture, and she mentored other women.

The fourth-century scholar Jerome wrote of her biblical scholarship:

She was in the front line in condemning the heretics; she brought forth witnesses who earlier had been taught by them and later were set straight from their heretical error. She showed how many of them had been deceived… she called upon the heretics in frequent letters to defend themselves.[2]

Paula the Elder

Paula (347–404) was another aristocrat, who came to faith after the death of her husband and was a member of the group led by

Marcella. She used her considerable wealth to build hospitals and care for the poor and to purchase ancient manuscripts to use in Bible translation. She and a group of friends travelled to the holy land, and she established several monastic communities near Bethlehem, including the first convent for women in the Western Church. The communities contained women from different social levels, and Paula worked hard to erase class distinctions, improve relationships and build up monastic life.

Having learned Greek from her father, Paula learned Hebrew from Jerome and worked with him on the earliest Western translation of the whole Bible. In his tribute to her after her death, Jerome cites many occasions when Paula's spiritual wisdom and faith exceeded his.

Macrina the Younger

Macrina (327–379) was born to Christian parents in Cappadocia and grew up in Pontus. She was betrothed at the age of twelve to a young man who died before they married; she vowed to remain single. She was well educated, which was unusual for the time, and, recognizing her potential, her brother Basil (who was later to become a bishop) arranged for her to receive education in theology.

In 355, while still in her 20s, Macrina founded a religious community for women on the family estate in Pontus, which was the model for other monasteries and convents. She insisted that the community support itself, and she herself lived a life of simplicity. She used money inherited from her parents to found a hospital to care for the poor and needy, and she was known for her holy life, her intellect and her teaching ability; many sought her out for spiritual counsel.

Women who believed they had a vocation to the religious life could exercise considerable autonomy within the confines of a monastic community. Although all women in orders depended on a priest for spiritual direction and the mass, women could exercise considerable leadership and influence as abbesses and prioresses. Our next examples come from the British Isles.

CELTIC AND ANGLO-SAXON ABBESSES

Brigid

Brigid (also known as Bride or Bridget) was born around 451, during the early years of the Celtic mission in Ireland. Her father was a tribal king and her mother a Christian bondwoman. When Brigid was 14, her father tried to marry her to a local noble, but she refused, opting instead to be a nun in the nearby monastery in Kildare.

She went on to become the abbess, and under her leadership the monastery was a place of Christian light in the midst of the druid darkness around it. The light at the centre of the community remained burning for a thousand years, until the monasteries were dissolved in the time of Henry VIII.

Brigid's life was written in the middle of the seventh century, and is the earliest life of an Irish saint. Stories about her suggest that she was strongwilled and determined but also very compassionate, and although some of the stories may be apocryphal, she is honoured alongside Patrick as one of Ireland's great evangelists and leaders. She died in about 525.

Hilda and Ebba

Like Brigid, Hilda was born into a royal family. She was baptized at the age of 13, in 627, and was encouraged by the Irish monk Aidan, who led the Celtic Christian mission to Northumbria from his base on Lindisfarne, to enter the religious life. Another woman, Ebba (who gives her name to a well-known church in Oxford), had founded a convent at Coldingham near Berwick in about 640, and Aidan encouraged Hilda to found another one, for both men and women, at Hartlepool. Not long afterwards, she founded another near Tadcaster and then moved to Whitby, where she founded a monastery, the community for which she is most famous. Bede writes of her:

So great was her prudence that not only ordinary folk, but kings and princes used to come and ask her advice in their difficulties and take it. Those under her direction were required to make a thorough study of the Scriptures and occupy themselves in good works, to such good effect that many were found fitted for Holy Orders and the service of God's altar.[3]

The community at Whitby acted as a training ground for clergy and was the place where the famous Synod was held in 664 to decide the direction of the British church. It may be because the church moved in a Roman rather than Celtic direction that women seem to have had less of a place as leaders in it after this point. As well as being a leader, Hilda is also remembered in tradition for her 'motherliness', thus combining the motherly and managerial in a way that we still struggle to bring together.

THE MIDDLE AGES

Hildegard of Bingen

The monastic life fostered women's talents, allowing some who chose this path to exercise their leadership gifts and permitting them the time, resources and status to produce other work. Until the 14th century, a religious community was the only place in which a woman would find a library.

The Benedictine abbess Hildegard of Bingen (1098–1179) was one of the most admired women of the Middle Ages. In recent years she has been 'rediscovered', mainly through her music, of which around 80 compositions survive. She is the first composer for whom a biography exists. Hildegard also wrote theological, botanical, medicinal and dietary texts, and also letters, poems and the first morality play.

She was also a leader. From her childhood she experienced visions and, probably as a result, she was placed in a small nunnery. On the death of the sister in charge, Hildegard was unanimously elected as 'magistra' or leader of the community. From there, 20 members moved in 1150 to her newly formed double monastery at Bingen, where she became abbess, exercising leadership over both men and women. Popes, bishops and kings as well as abbots and abbesses looked to her for prayers and advice on various matters, and she travelled widely during four preaching tours, the only woman known to have done so at this time. No feminist, Hildegard insisted that her influence exposed the lacklustre nature of the clergy: only in dire necessity would God have resorted to her!

Catherine of Siena

Catherine (1347–80) was, from a young age, drawn to the religious life. She overcame family opposition to her vocation and in 1363 joined the Third Order of the Dominicans. While she wished to live a life of spiritual discipline, her desire to exercise the religious life in an active way drew her to care for the poor of Siena, and she attracted followers by her example.

As she saw the corruption of public life around her, she felt impelled to speak out, denouncing greed and spiritual poverty and challenging the Pope himself. Seeing that God was calling her to a more public leadership role, she went to Avignon to confront the Pope, urging him to return to Rome and deal with the problems in the Church. Catherine wrote a *Dialogue* on the spiritual life, as well as numerous letters of counsel and direction.

THE REFORMATION

The Reformation that swept through Europe in the 15th–16th centuries had varying effects on the role of women as leaders in the Church. As religious houses were dissolved, the monks could fulfil their religious vocations as parish priests, but women had no such place in the new system. Some of the reformers, such as Martin Luther and John Calvin, continued to assume the spiritual inferiority of women, yet some women emerged as leaders, particularly in movements that were more radically egalitarian. In these, spiritual gifting was often regarded as more important than tradition or authorization.

The Lollards

The Reformation was anticipated in England by a small group of men and women called the Lollards. They followed the writings and ideas of John Wycliff (c.1329–84), a radical Oxford theologian, who initiated a new translation of the Latin Vulgate Bible into English. They were held together by common beliefs and practices that included radical equality. There were no ordained leaders among the group but they believed that all believers, including women, could interpret, teach and preach the word of God.

There were a number of women in the group, who defended their position as preachers by looking to female prophets in the Bible and to references to prophecy (which was clearly, in the New Testament, open to women). From the beginning the Lollards were suppressed, especially when they were seen as a political threat. Sybil Godsell, who was tried for heresy in Norwich, is reported to have said, 'Every faithful man and every faithful woman is a good priest and has as good power to make the body of Christ as any ordained priest.'[4]

Margaret Fell and the Quakers

Margaret Fell was a remarkable woman and played a significant role in the formation of Quakerism. Born in 1614, she married Thomas Fell, a judge and prominent member of society. Margaret heard George Fox preach in 1652 and invited him to visit her home at Swarthmoor Hall in Lancashire. From this time, Swarthmore Hall became the headquarters of the movement, with Margaret leading through her hospitality, travelling, speaking, letter writing and pamphlets.

George Fox had remarkably egalitarian views. When he encountered men who believed that women had no souls, he reminded them of Mary's words, 'My soul doth magnify the Lord' (Luke 1:46, KJV). On one occasion he was angered when he observed a woman ask a question in church, only to be told by the priest that he did not permit women to speak in church.

The group's beliefs were similar to those of the Lollards, and they believed in the equality of all people before God. They sought to base their practice on the early Church, seeing that all people were prophets and that all people were called to ministry. The revival movement was thus, like the Lollards, very attractive to women; so many women were involved in the initial stages of Quakerism that it was rumoured to be a women's cult. During the 1640s and '50s, women were teaching, preaching, leading worship and evangelizing on an unprecedented scale, with Margaret Fell as a key leader behind it all.

In 1666, while imprisoned in Lancaster Castle for holding religious meetings, Margaret wrote *Women's Speaking Justified* (a short version of the typically snappy title *Women's Speaking Justified, Proved and Allowed of by the Scriptures, All such as speak by the Spirit and Power of the Lord Jesus. And how Women were the first that Preached the Tidings of the Resurrection of Jesus, and were sent by Christ's own Command, before he ascended to the Father, John 20:17*). This was the first book by a woman since the Reformation to plead for recognition of the spiritual equality of men and women.

The book draws on arguments such as women preaching the message of the resurrection, the role of Priscilla in teaching Apollos, and women in the Old Testament such as Deborah, Huldah and Sarah, and it tackles the passages in Paul (1 Corinthians 14 and 1 Timothy 2) that might appear to restrict women's ministry. She argued that opposition to women's speaking came from the spirit of darkness and apostasy that had been prevailing in the Church for 1200 years: 'So let this serve to stop that opposing Spirit that would limit the Power and Spirit of the Lord Jesus, whose Spirit is poured upon all Flesh, both Sons and Daughters, now in his Resurrection.'[5]

The danger of the loosely organized movement was that it was at risk of people on the fringe giving it a bad name. As a result of breakaway movements like the Ranters, and the danger of persecution, George Fox and Margaret (whom he married in 1669, after her first husband's death) worked on an organization for the fledgling movement.

This had advantages: groups of Quakers met together in a more organized way and women exercised leadership over groups of other women. In one of Margaret's letters of 1697, she refers to a group of women called 'ministers'—in other words, preachers. For 30 years, Margaret and her daughters, many of whom were among the next generation of Quaker leaders, worked to create women's meetings.

In the long run, however, separate women's meetings spelled the end for real equality. By the beginning of the 18th century there was a marked decline in the activity of women in the Quakers. This pattern is often repeated: women have significant leadership roles at the beginning of new movements but are pushed into the background once they become more organized. Nevertheless, the legacy of the Quakers was considerable, including the initial move to abolish the slave trade, campaigning for women's suffrage (in the USA), and pioneering higher education for women.

Baptists

Baptist churches have existed in Britain since the early 17th century and women played a prominent role from the beginning. Women preached, taught, founded churches and took part in church meetings. Their heritage was from the radical churches of the Anabaptists on the continent, and they were part of the reforming wing of the Church that emphasized the priesthood of all believers.

The best-known female preacher from this period is perhaps Mrs Attaway, who preached to more than a thousand people in London each Tuesday afternoon in 1645. Three other prominent women—Catherine Sutton, Anne Hempstall and Mary Bilbrowe—all faced persecution but continued to speak and lead. Dorothy Hazzard (d. 1674) led the way in founding the congregation that became Broadmead Baptist Church in Bristol. Sadly, in the next century, women were unable to have so public a role within Baptist churches, at least at home, but the mission movement of the 19th century gave Baptist women more scope again for public ministry and leadership. In 1925, the Baptist Union Council officially accepted the call of women to pastorates.

THE 18TH CENTURY

Wesleyan revival

It was among the followers of John Wesley, whose movement was initially a revival within the Anglican Church, that women's preaching resurfaced, following the same pattern as in the Quaker and Baptist movements.

It has become fashionable in the last few years to speak of the 'feminization' of the Church, implying that churches with significantly more women than men, and women in leadership, will deter men. However, Christianity from the beginning, and in most periods of revival, has attracted more women than men, and this was the case with Wesley's movement. It soon became apparent that more women than men were attracted by his teaching. From 1742 women could be class (small group) leaders and led solely female 'classes'. These proved an ideal ground for women to train in leadership and preaching. Many women who became preachers did so by taking progressive steps of authority within the system: recruiting others to attend meetings, leading a class, and then 'warming and exhorting people'—in other words, preaching.

It was due to the leadership qualities of many of these women that the class meetings they organized kept growing, and more people came to them seeking instruction in the new faith. Sarah Crosby wrote to Wesley in 1761, explaining that 200 people had come to one of her class meetings and she was uncertain of how to continue.

I was not sure whether it was right for me to exhort in so public a manner, and yet I saw it impracticable to meet all these people by way of speaking particularly to each individual. I, therefore, gave out a hymn and prayed, and told them part of what the Lord had done for me, persuading them to flee from all sin.[6]

Wesley's qualified approval of Sarah Crosby's actions marks the beginning of his acceptance of women preachers. In 1777 Crosby rode 960 miles, held 220 public and 600 private meetings, and wrote 116 letters. While we could say that she was 'only' a preacher, it is clear that she was also one of the leaders of the revival.

Another leader was Grace Murray: 'Mr Wesley made me a Leader of a Band; I was afraid of undertaking it, yet durst not refuse, lest I offend God.' She was responsible for meetings with classes, visiting the sick and those who were backsliding, and travelling to other societies, including, in Ireland, acting in effect as a sub-pastor. Wesley referred to her as 'servant and friend, and fellow-labourer in the gospel'.[7]

Elizabeth Tonkin followed in the footsteps of another woman who was her mentor, and emerged as clear leader of a Methodist work in

Cornwall, where she arranged the meetings and organized who the preachers would be. One night when the preacher did not turn up, she was pressed by the congregation to preach and reluctantly did so, the power of God coming down. For nearly 20 years she held meetings and preached in her local area.

Wesley's solution to this was to see women's preaching as an 'extraordinary' call in the midst of revival. Admittedly there were too many women involved for it to be extraordinary, but this was how he squared women's leadership with what he thought scripture said. The number of women preachers increased and their influence was felt right across the country. There were at least 27 well-known women preachers.

Wesley was certainly influenced by his mother, who grew up in a Puritan home and taught herself Hebrew, Greek and Latin in her teens so that she could read the Bible in the original languages. When her vicar husband was absent, she invited people into her home and the congregation grew rapidly under her leadership. She believed that obedience to the Spirit was more important than obedience to the state Church—and this stress on inner conviction has been a significant feature of the ministry of women leaders.

As the number of women looked set to continue growing, Wesley died, in 1791. With his strong leadership no longer holding the Methodists together, the movement began to disintegrate into different groups. The largest was the Wesleyan Methodists and, as this was consolidated around the turn of the century, women preachers were repressed. The 1803 Conference called the preaching of women into question, branding it both 'unnecessary' and 'generally undesirable'.

Women's preaching remained strongest wherever smaller groups resisted institutionalization—for example, among the Primitive Methodists—and recent research has found that there were at least 200 women preachers within these groups. Slowly, even the smaller sections of Methodism yielded to the pressure to conform. Chapels were built and, as formerly persecuted sects became respected denominations and men were trained and authorized for ministry, women were excluded. By 1869, in the London Primitive Methodists there were only eleven female local preachers, as opposed to 432 men.

There was just enough memory for the mantle to be passed on to another group of women—those who emerged in the mid-19th-century revival. Before that, however, we meet two women who had considerable leadership influence, both in distinctive and different ways.

Selina, Countess of Huntingdon

Selina, Countess of Huntingdon (1707–91), resolved to use her position and wealth for the sake of the gospel. She became a protector and supporter of Wesley and Whitefield when they encountered opposition. In 1760 she opened a chapel in Brighton, the first of many, and it is estimated that 100,000 people heard the gospel in the 60 chapels that she founded.

Church planting on this scale threatened the status quo, and the new congregations became dissenting chapels with her name attached—hence the 'Countess of Huntingdon's Connexion', which still has 20 congregations in England and some in Sierra Leone. She also founded a college to train ministers and functioned much like a medieval abbess, visiting chapels to oversee the work and taking charge of the pastoral training and finance.

Hannah More

Jilted at the altar at the age of 28, Hannah More (1745–1833) turned her considerable abilities to blazing a trail for women. Educational pioneer, playwright, social reformer and friend to many, she was one of the first to see the need for schools to reach all levels of society. She used her leadership talent to open schools in Cheddar and other villages in the Mendips, start benefit clubs for women, and bring Christian influence to the local communities. Church attendance soared, women and children learned to read the Bible, and the area witnessed a mini-revival. Her writing of 'Cheap Repository Tracts' led to the formation of the Religious Tract Society in 1799.

Like most people of her day, Hannah More believed in sexual differentiation and she was convinced that women had a civilizing effect. 'The Old Bishop in Petticoats', William Cobbett called her— but she was an influential leader, both within her own wide circles and as a role model for other women. She was the first in a whole line of evangelical women philanthropists who were to change the shape of social welfare in Britain.

19TH-CENTURY REVIVAL

It is no coincidence that the issue of women as preachers in the Church was taken up again in the 1860s, at the time when the effects of the Second Evangelical Awakening in America (1800–40) were beginning to be felt in England. There were outbursts of spontaneous revival in Cornwall and North Devon, parts of Scotland and Ulster, while in England itself the revival was more organized, based on the new wave of revival teaching stemming from Charles Grandison Finney in his published *Lectures on Revivals of Religion*.

Finney encouraged social reform, which included the elevation of women, and he allowed women to pray aloud and testify in mixed gatherings. Because of his encouragement, women felt empowered to play their part in spreading the good news publicly.

As befitted the culture of mid-Victorian respectability, the open-air preaching of past revivals was replaced by meetings in hired halls, and the key preachers came from the respectable middle class—but they were still lay people, not ordained. A new generation of women preachers rose up, for just a decade, but on a more publicized scale than before and with greater respectability. These women recognized their debt to women preachers of the past, in particular the Methodists.

Phoebe Palmer

Phoebe Palmer (1807–74) came to prominence in the American revival. She was a middle-class woman from a Methodist family, married to a doctor in New York. Early in her married life she experienced a period of intense spiritual struggle because, like many brought up in Christian homes, she believed she had had no conversion experience. Her struggle led her to a new version of 'holiness' teaching: that if a person made a decision to give all to Christ—or, in her terminology, 'lay all upon' God's 'altar', which was Christ—they became sanctified, because Christ was holy and 'whatsoever toucheth the altar shall be holy'. Phoebe made this decision for sanctification in 1837 and then began to share her new conviction with others.

Her sister had started a class meeting in Phoebe's house when she had come for a long visit, and Phoebe had taken over its leadership when her sister left. It was originally an all-women's group but, just like her Methodist predecessors, Palmer found that it soon grew to include interested men, and it eventually became a group of some 300 people. As others heard about the teaching, Palmer was invited to speak elsewhere and she soon found she was becoming a popular itinerant preacher.

She wrote two books to explain her beliefs: *The Way of Holiness* (1843) and *Entire Devotion to God* (1845). Her books had an even wider audience than her preaching and were sold overseas, especially in Britain. Soon Phoebe Palmer was invited to come to Britain to preach and she arrived in 1859, staying for four years. She toured the country with her husband, preaching 'pardon and purity', chiefly in Methodist chapels, and influencing many others. Her meetings were characterized by deep emotion and power. Thousands were converted and added to the churches.

At first, Phoebe Palmer had misgivings about the appropriateness of her position as a female preacher but she became convinced that she had been divinely called. Her evident success was not enough to explain her calling to others, however, and she wrote a book to defend the preaching of women. This was published in Boston in 1859, entitled *The Promise of the Father, or A neglected speciality of the last days*. The main title gives a clear indication of Palmer's argument—that women were present on the day of Pentecost, were anointed by the Holy Spirit, and prophesied along with their fellow (male) disciples. This fulfilled the prophecy of Joel quoted by Peter, that God had poured out his Spirit on his sons and daughters in the last days. Palmer argued that, since preaching and prophecy were the same thing, women's 'preaching' was biblically sanctioned.

Palmer challenged prevailing views of what women should do and be, and became a role model for Catherine Booth (co-founder of the Salvation Army) and other revival preachers. But Palmer was also hesitant to step too far beyond what was expected. She was hesitant to describe her own actions as 'preaching': she referred to her sermon as a 'talk', and often spoke after a normal service had taken place. Like most preaching wives, she worked with her husband, spoke only from the steps of the pulpit and often refrained from publishing works in her own name. However, she set an example that others soon followed. Nearly 40 of these women have been traced in some detail, and the most successful of them drew huge crowds. In this era some preachers had the same kind of drawing power and influence as music stars or other celebrities today.

It seems that holiness teaching had a particular appeal to women, so that they often became prominent where the movement flourished. The exhortation to 'lay all on the altar' would have helped women who felt called to preach to disregard human rules in favour of obeying God.

By the 1870s, Christians converted in the revival were being incorporated into churches, and this period was much less favourable to women's ministry. Assemblies began to acquire their own halls.

Many who could accept women as preachers, prophets and evangelists were not willing to accept them as pastors and teachers or leaders within churches. It appears, too, that many of the women were keen to defend their preaching but were less concerned about women's leadership of congregations. The process of institutionalization had begun again, and women were reduced to an ancillary role.

Catherine Booth

Phoebe Palmer was a formative influence on Catherine Booth, who went on with her husband William to found the Salvation Army. Reared in a strict Methodist home, Catherine had read the Bible ten times by the age of twelve. But apart from the occasional female class meeting leader, she would have seen few women in places of responsibility and fewer still preaching the gospel—until the arrival of Phoebe Palmer in Britain.

Palmer came under attack from those who disagreed with her actions, and Catherine Booth decided to go into print to defend her. She wrote a pamphlet, *Female Ministry; or Women's Right to Preach the Gospel* (1860). It is clear from her choice of title that she believed that women had a right to minister and preach, and her writing was radical compared with that of Palmer. She argued that women were not unfit for the task as some opponents had argued, but that they were naturally very well suited by their 'graceful form and attitude, winning manners, persuasive speech, and above all, a finely-toned emotional nature'.[8]

In contrast with Phoebe Palmer, Booth did not argue that women should be associated with the domestic sphere, and wrote that if men had been freed from the curse of working in the field, then women should be freed from being confined exclusively to the kitchen. She then turned to the Bible passages often used in connection with women's preaching. Her arguments drew on her conviction that the first coming of Christ had made gender irrelevant in the Church. As

Palmer argued, she recognized that on the day of Pentecost women prophesied, and that this was also the case in Corinth. The question was not whether they should do so but 'whether, as a matter of convenience, they might do so without their veils'. On the passage in 1 Timothy 2, she argued that it should read, 'I suffer not a woman to teach by usurping authority over a man',[9] and concluded that women should be permitted to preach so long as they did it in a fitting way. If a woman was gifted and called to preach, she should do so. It is clear from this that Catherine Booth had more in common with the Quaker tradition of equality than with the Methodist line that women's preaching was an exception to an otherwise binding rule.

Women's proper influence

When it came to marriage, Catherine was convinced that she would only marry a man who was committed to female ministry, not just in theory but in practice—even though she herself had not yet preached. William, at the invitation of a friend, heard the preaching in London of a woman called Miss Buck. He was so impressed that he vowed never again to oppose women's preaching. A letter Catherine wrote to him just before she married states that she is convinced of the true and scriptural character of her views on women's ministry.

I believe woman is destined to assume her true position and exert her proper influence by the special exertions and attainments of her own sex... May the Lord, even the just and impartial One, overrule all for the true emancipation of women from the swaddling bands of prejudice, ignorance and custom, which, almost the world over, have so long debased and wronged her.[10]

She argued that the mistaken application of the passage 'Let the women keep silence in the churches' 'has resulted in more loss to the Church, evil to the world and dishonour to God than any other errors we have already referred to'.[11]

From the moment Catherine began preaching in 1860, her ministry grew. When William had a breakdown in the summer of that year, she took over all the preaching in his Methodist circuit and was so successful that they asked her to continue and share the work when her husband recovered. When the Booths left the Methodists in order to follow their sense of calling, they were invited as evangelists to speak at many missions together. They soon realized that they could reach more people if they split up and ministered separately. Once William started his mission work in the East End of London, it was Catherine who was the breadwinner, remaining in itinerant preaching, spreading the news of the mission and raising funds. She was committed to being a wife and mother (she had eight children) as well as a leader, but it was as a preacher on the platform or in a Salvation Army corps that, by her own admission, she felt most at home.

In 1870 William Booth laid down in the constitution of his Christian Mission the principle that women have an equal standing with men as publishers of salvation to the world. In 1878 this reappeared in the founding statutes of the Salvation Army. In 1880 two training homes were created to equip the new leaders, one for men and one for women. The Army set up centres around the country for evangelism and work among the poor, and in 1876 it was decided that women could be overall leaders of these stations, not just assistants.

By 1878 there were 30 women 'in the field', by 1883 there were 723 male officers and 746 female officers, and in 1900 40 per cent of the Army's officers were said to be women. Their 'Major Barbaras' and 'Hallelujah Lasses', as they were popularly known, helped people to recognize that women could teach, organize and lead.

Ellen Ranyard: leading mission to the poor

One of my favourite leadership heroes is Ellen Ranyard (1810–79), who was the pioneer of the London Bible and Domestic Female

Mission (or Ranyard Bible Mission, as it came to be known), a new movement to evangelize working-class women in London. Inspired by the missionary use of 'native agency', she struck on the idea of selling Bibles to the poor, using other working-class women. In 1859 she published *The Missing Link*, arguing that 'Bible-women' were the 'missing link' between the working poor and the gospel.

The role of these agents was to encourage women to buy Bibles. The key to the whole approach was personal contact. They invited the women to a meeting with others in the agent's home to discuss self-improvement, family and domestic matters: many of the women had drunken husbands who did not provide adequately for their families, and women had to manage as best they could. The third stage was to invite them to the society-run mission room for teaching by a 'sister in Christ', with a view to joining a local congregation. We might well see this as an effective (and more holistic?) forerunner of today's 'process evangelism' approaches.

Ranyard's approach captured the attention and support of middle-class evangelicals and the mission made astonishing progress, the result of her remarkable vision and hard work. By 1860, 137 Bible women were employed—women from working-class backgrounds who were the key to Ranyard's remarkable strategy.

By 1867 there were 234 Bible women, and in the following year Ranyard arranged for the training of poor women as itinerant nurses in the wards of Guy's Hospital—one of the earliest examples of district nursing in London. The visionary leadership of this remarkable woman produced grassroots person-to-person evangelism, something like the first social workers, and early district nursing.

Mary Sumner: an accidental leader?

Mary Sumner probably never intended to become the leader of a large organization, which soon became worldwide. The wife of a clergyman, she realized the importance of mothers bringing up their children within the Christian faith. When her own children had grown up, she started to invite younger mothers to the rectory to explore parenting skills and encourage them to pass on their faith. Several years later, at a church congress in 1885, Sumner spoke of the opportunities that women had to bring up their children in the faith, and the Mothers' Union was founded.

Sumner's idea of women was a traditional one: their place was in the home, bringing up children and training them for their future place in society. But the Mothers' Union gave leadership potential to many women, who found themselves leading other women in local branches. In parts of the Church where the MU is strong, especially in Africa, it is still a powerful training ground for women leaders.

This raises the issue of whether leadership in an all-women organization is good in the long run or counterproductive in terms of a goal of leadership partnership for men and women. We might also ask whether the MU's emphasis on women's role in spiritual nurture unhelpfully pushes the responsibility for bringing up children away from women *and* men (see Deuteronomy 32:46; Proverbs 1:8, 4:3–4) on to women, and reinforces traditional roles for women in the Church. This may be a danger, but the organization, especially in the developing world, has provided positive opportunities for women to lead and helped women to gain improved health care and educational opportunities for themselves and their children.

Frances Willard: leading for abolition and temperance

Frances Willard (1839–98) was both a preacher and a leader. Born in New York, she became a teacher after graduating from college. In 1873 she took up the post of Dean of Women at the Women's College of Northwestern University in Chicago.

Converted at a Methodist revival meeting in her early 20s, she joined the Methodist Church. Her faith soon led her to involvement not only in mission but also in temperance work, which was one of the few viable public ministries for women in the 19th century. She was involved in founding and later leading the Women's Christian Temperance Union, the largest 19th-century women's organization in the world, which promoted evangelistic work in prisons and workplaces and worked for the abolition of slavery, women's suffrage and temperance around the world. From 1874 she travelled widely, averaging 30,000 miles and 400 lectures a year. She crossed the Atlantic a number of times, thus influencing women in Britain as well as America.

Willard was invited to work with evangelist Dwight Moody, preaching and speaking at his meetings. By the 1880s she was openly demanding an equal role for women in the Church and she wrote *Woman in the Pulpit* (1888) to look at arguments for the preaching of women and to refute counter-arguments. The book challenges a literal interpretation of scripture inconsistently applied, and assumes that scripture should be used to interpret scripture. Her work challenged women to use their gifts alongside men: 'Let me, as a loyal daughter of the church, urge upon younger women who feel a call, as I once did, to preach the unsearchable riches of Christ.'[12] Willard inspired other women to assume leadership in evangelism and social action.

LEADING IN MISSION

The 19th century saw the expansion of the missionary movement, and Christian women were drawn to overseas mission. Often, this involved joining a women's mission, where they could assume leadership and acquire skills they might not have gained otherwise. Perhaps mission was the place where women were most free to use their gifts—and many early women missionaries were pioneers in many different ways.

In the first half of the 19th century, the Church Missionary Society was the first to send single women to the mission field. By the 1860s it was becoming commonplace for single women to serve as overseas missionaries, and many of those who did so trained as teachers, nurses or deaconesses. In 1876 Mary Slessor began her mission work in West Africa, and she in turn became a role model for other women.

An important result of the mid-century revival was the founding of a large number of interdenominational missions operating on the 'faith' principle (asking God to provide rather than asking for funds for the work). The largest of these was the China Inland Mission (CIM) founded by James Hudson Taylor, who was unusually open to women's ministry. The CIM became a model for many other societies. As they were interdenominational, emphasis on ordination was less important; what counted was (in the words of Emma Bevan) 'the mighty ordination of the pierced hands'. However, when women returned home, many of them were unable to speak in public on deputation tours, and this strange discrepancy persisted until recently.

Women were trained for overseas mission in Bible colleges and institutes and began to gain skills in exegesis and Bible interpretation. This meant that, as well as being equipped for evangelism, they developed new skills for challenging interpretations of scripture that hindered their participation in leadership and mission. This in turn gave them confidence to use their gifts, and, having worked together, especially in the USA, to gain the right to vote and abolish slavery, they showed that they could achieve great things and (literally) set people free. Patterns of shared leadership began to emerge where women were involved. Women's intellectual, moral and spiritual leadership on mission fields around the globe provided a challenge to the long-held assumptions that they could not do these things because of their supposed inferiority.

The first women's missionary society (with the good Victorian name 'The Society for Promoting Female Education in the East') was founded in 1834, aiming to help single women to enter the mission field and start schools for girls overseas. This society was followed by many others, and women began to develop an informal interdenominational network that became known as the 'women's missionary movement'. This network helped to develop women's mission agencies, and thousands of women were sent out from Europe and the USA while millions on the 'home front' supported them. Early in the 20th century, it seemed logical for women's societies to cooperate more fully with the other longstanding societies, since arguably it would be more fruitful to be united. However, most male leaders were not ready to work with women as equals and men assumed all the leadership positions.

Pandita Ramabai: leader for justice

Pandita Ramabai (1858–1922) was a remarkable Indian woman who founded a mission to reach India's neglected child-widows and became the pre-eminent pioneer of women's rights in that country. She was born into a Brahmin (highest, or priestly, Hindu caste) family and her father defied social custom by giving his daughter an education. He also refused to arrange her marriage. Tragically, her father, mother and sister died from starvation during a famine in 1874–76, leaving Ramabai and her brother on their own, and they eventually arrived in Calcutta. As a 20-year-old woman, Ramabai amazed the people of Calcutta with her knowledge of Sanskrit and ancient texts, becoming an instant celebrity; they honoured her with the title *Pandita*, which means 'wise person'. She married in 1880 but her husband died and she was left to raise their daughter on her own.

Troubled by the suffering she saw around her, Ramabai established herself as a champion of the oppressed—especially women. In 1883 she went to study medicine in England and came into contact with an Anglican religious community at Wantage. When the sisters encouraged her to read the New Testament, she was deeply touched by the person of Jesus, especially the way he treated the oppressed. She started to realize that Christ could transform and uplift the downtrodden women of India.

Ramabai was baptized into the Christian faith but remained a cultural Hindu and was sometimes misunderstood by people of both faiths. Invited to the USA, she met some of the early women's rights leaders and, in 1887, published her book *The High-Caste Hindu Woman*, the first Indian feminist manifesto. In it she outlined the plight of Brahmin women, who were often widowed while still children, blamed for their husbands' deaths and treated as outcasts. In 1899 she founded the Mukti (Salvation) Mission, which ministered to women and girls who were in need, eventually growing to house and educate over 2000 girls and women.

Among her other achievements, she translated the entire Bible from the original Hebrew and Greek into her native Marathi—the only Bible translation done completely by a woman. Ramabai was a strong leader with a clear vision; she refused to conform to the norms of her society or the way women were expected to act.

Amy Carmichael

Amy Carmichael was born in Northern Ireland to Presbyterian parents. Despite suffering from neuralgia, a painful disorder of the nerves, which frequently incapacitated her, and a fall in 1931 which confined her to bed, she exercised a remarkable and influential ministry. At the Keswick Convention she heard God call her to mission and left England in 1890, at the age of 23, to go to the Far East. Her first assignment was in Japan but she did not settle well, and in 1895 she started work in India, where she would spend the rest of her life. In 1901 she rescued a child from temple prostitution and so began her ministry of rescuing girls from this life, establishing a home and school for them at Dohnavur. She served in India for 55 years and died there in 1951. In the last 20 years of her life she wrote 13 books and updated those written earlier; many of them are still in print. The Dohnavur Fellowship continues to thrive over 50 years after her death.

HOLINESS AND REVIVAL MOVEMENTS

The Keswick Convention, where Amy Carmichael received her call, institutionalized the holiness revival of the earlier 19th century and was held annually from 1876. It drew people from across the denominations. Women gave public Bible readings with comments, and Jessie Penn Lewis (1862–1927), a holiness preacher, teacher and theologian from a Methodist background, was a regular speaker and an advocate of biblical equality for women. She initiated a Keswick convention in Wales in 1903, chronicled the Welsh revival in *Life of Faith* magazine and founded *The Overcomer* magazine. Unfortunately, she came to hold some unorthodox views later in her life and this contributed to the revival's demise.

Other women are known to have played a prominent part in the Welsh revival (1904–05). Evan Roberts, one of the key leaders, supported and encouraged women's ministry; many women preached and some led teams to other parts of Britain. Like so many revival movements, the Welsh revival was marked by factors that have traditionally made it easier for women to take a leadership role: they took the promise of Acts 2:17–18 literally, it was a grassroots revival led by non-professionals, and the meetings were informal and Spirit-led. After the revival, however, women were again silenced by male clergy.

Early Pentecostals

Women also played a key part in the Pentecostal revival in Britain. The Pentecostal League was founded in 1891 by Reader Harris and his wife Mary. Its aim was the filling of the Holy Spirit for all believers, revival for the churches and the spread of scriptural holiness. By 1900 it had 17,000 members and 150 networked prayer groups all over Britain, many of which were led by women. When Harris died in 1909, the leadership went to Mary, a preacher and teacher, who later became head of Ridgelands Bible College, London. The first person to be baptized in the Holy Spirit and speak in tongues in connection with the 20th-century outpouring was Catherine Price, a Londoner who became part of the inner circle of leaders in the early days of the revival.

It is often forgotten that the revival in the UK started in the Anglican Church. Mary Boddy, wife of the vicar of Monkswearmouth, Sunderland, was an invalid but was healed and subsequently exercised a remarkable healing and speaking ministry around the country. At the first Convention of the revival, held in Sunderland in 1908, gender divisions were swept away and women were able to exercise their gifts freely. Alexander Boddy believed Acts 2:17–18, that God's Spirit was poured out on all people, which meant that 'daughters will prophesy', and he operated an equal opportunities policy in ministry and leadership.

Other influential women leaders in the Pentecostal revival included Margaret Cantel, who was involved in the formation of Assemblies of God in 1924; Christina Beruldsen, a church planter who opened a mission at Leith Docks; Eleanor Crisp, principal of the women's Pentecostal Missionary Union training college, who moulded a generation of women who served overseas as missionaries; and Polly Wigglesworth, a born leader and excellent preacher married to the famous Smith Wigglesworth. With him she exercised an itinerant preaching and healing ministry.

Sadly, in 1914, one topic on the agenda at the annual Convention was 'A woman's place in the Church'. As the Pentecostal movement became institutionalized, the issue of women's place was decided— as so often—by men.

THE STORY CONTINUES

At the time of the mid-19th-century revival, there was a lively debate about women's role in churches, with contributions from both sides of the Atlantic showing that female preaching was in accordance with both God's will and the practice of the early Church. Numerous pamphlets on female preaching appeared in Britain between 1864 and 1866, following Catherine Booth's of 1859.

By the end of the century, however, except in the Salvation Army, no woman could hope to attain a leadership role. Gifts of teaching and preaching were restricted to non-worship and often totally female settings. Most men in leadership roles in churches and church-related organizations were unable to concede that there were good scriptural precedents for the full ministry of women. Not just scriptural arguments but also the influence of the 'ideal Christian woman' (the 'angel in the house', a modest homemaker) meant that, in the Church of England, women could not even vote in Parochial Church Councils when they were established in 1897, and, when the House of Laymen was set up in 1903, women were excluded from being participants or even electors.

However, women had begun to find their own way in wider society. Now better educated, their capabilities had been proved in many spheres. They were seen to be effective preachers and evangelists, and they served as nurses in the terrible conditions of the Crimean war, as deaconesses in slums, and in the expanding missionary societies. The evangelical emphasis on the priesthood of all believers was a strength, giving women confidence to know that they had a part to play. They were willing to serve in the background or to step up to leadership if needed.

The fundamentalist controversy in the USA early in the 20th century, and its aftermath, resulted in some evangelicals putting renewed emphasis on the inspiration or infallibility of scripture as they saw it, and some leadership and preaching roles for women were limited by appeal to 1 Corinthians 14 and 1 Timothy 2. By the 1950s, women were no longer viewed as equal partners with men in ministry and service. In addition, post-war prosperity and the baby boom created a new paradigm that reconfirmed women as keepers of the domestic front. This in turn spurred the feminist movement of the 1960s and a variety of responses from the Church.

'God, through his daughters here, is taking aim'[13]

The story of women leaders through 2000 years of church history shows, sadly, how their lives and calling have been constrained by man-made rules. While women have begun to emerge into new roles in wider society, in some churches they are still hindered by old prejudices, old interpretations, old assumptions. Many women are still restricted to leading other women and some will never see women leaders at work in the Church.

But for those with eyes to see what God has done, there are many role models. As church leader and consultant Martin Robinson has said, 'It is astonishing how frequently women have been the ones to break barriers, forge new frontiers and advance the cause of the Gospel in fresh and surprising ways. Courage and tenacity matched only by creativity and grace were the hallmarks of these amazing leaders.'[14] These words were written about the women of the early Pentecostal revival, but could apply to all the women leaders whose stories we have considered here—and many more.

QUESTIONS FOR REFLECTION AND DISCUSSION

- Why do you think stories of women church leaders over the centuries are so little known today?
- Out of the women leaders in church history whom you know about, whom do you most admire? Why?

―――― Part 2 ――――

WAYS WOMEN LEAD

In Part 2 we turn to the question of how women lead. As women have begun to assume leadership roles that were traditionally occupied by men, many people have assumed that women will bring something 'different' to leadership. But is this true? Do women lead differently from the way men lead or are other factors at work? Before examining this, we need first to understand what leadership is, so Chapter 4 outlines the history of leadership as a concept, explores the distinctives of Christian leadership and summarizes current leadership thinking. Chapter 5 then looks at gender stereotypes and the 'difference' of women before using recent research to answer the fascinating question of how women lead.

✣

Chapter 4

A BRIEF HISTORY OF LEADERSHIP

'A leader is someone who makes a difference through influencing others…
Christian leaders seek to make a positive difference by influencing others
toward the purposes of God.'
ROBERTA HESTENES[1]

'We need to move from the leader as hero, to the leader as host.'
MARGARET WHEATLEY[2]

For as long as there have been people, there have been leaders.
Think of ancient burial mounds, the pyramids, Stonehenge. How did
those things happen? They all required planning, and lots of people.
Someone, or some people, took the lead in those accomplishments.
As we think about the Old Testament, the word 'leader' may not
be in our concordance but we can identity Moses, Deborah, David
and Nehemiah as leaders. Reflections on leadership can be found
in the writings of the Greeks, Romans and Chinese, and in Western
literature of the last 2000 years.

ARE LEADERS BORN OR MADE?

Study and research on the concept of leadership is relatively new,
starting in the early 20th century. People started to ask what made
some people great leaders, and the earliest theories were the 'great
man' (and they were men!) or 'trait' theories. Studies in the 1920s
assumed that effective leaders were born, not made, and set out to
ask what was great or special about them, what traits they had in

common. Leaders were seen as exceptional men who possessed innate characteristics such as intelligence, energy and dominance.

Attention turned in the 1940s from 'who leaders are' to 'what leaders do'. Research identified two essential aspects of leadership:

- providing clear instructions and directions (task-oriented)
- giving personal support and encouragement (relationship-oriented)

Focusing on these two types of behaviour was believed to make people good leaders; and this approach clearly favoured the idea that leaders are made rather than born.

Born or made? Maybe the truth lies somewhere in between. In the 1960s and '70s, thinking on leadership took a new direction— the view that leadership is situational: effective leadership involves doing the right thing at the right time. A good leader is one who is able to see what combination of task and relational behaviour will be most effective in any given situation.

TRANSACTIONAL OR TRANSFORMATIONAL?

From the 1970s onwards, thinkers on leadership began to see that leadership could be more than accomplishing a task by getting followers to do as the leader wished by means of a 'transaction', such as financial reward. Leaders who exercised 'transformational' (rather than transactional) leadership inspired those they led, and provided vision and meaning. They encouraged their followers to contribute to the solution, to be creative and innovative. They were more interested in understanding those they led.

At around this time John Adair, now one of the most respected thinkers on leadership, devised a much-used model that identified three strands of leadership: task, team and individual. Good leaders need to focus on all three but may need more emphasis on one of the strands according to the situation. Imagine a team leading the youth work in a church. There is a *task* to be done: growing young people in discipleship. This will be done more efficiently if the *team* members are doing what they do best, playing to their strengths, whether that is creative games, Bible knowledge or being a good listener. Furthermore, the overall leader knows that one *individual* on the team, Rachel, went to her grandad's funeral last week and is not feeling her best. The other leaders do a bit extra this week, working well together and supporting Rachel, so that the task is achieved.

Today, for a whole variety of reasons, old models of 'command and control', based on the idea that the leader knows best and has the right to give orders that followers are obliged to obey, are seen as outmoded. Instead, current writers on leadership see and affirm a much more collaborative, enabling model, in which the leader draws on people's gifts, skills and ideas to achieve the goal.[3]

UNDERSTANDING LEADERSHIP TODAY

With that brief overview, we can summarize our understanding of leadership by recognizing four ways of thinking about the subject today. The following aspects come from *Growing Leaders* by James Lawrence (BRF, 2004), but reflect widely recognized ways of thinking about leadership.

Leadership as function

We all exercise leadership to some extent. Anyone who has influence over another person is leading them. If you look at a group of children, perhaps your own, or in a group in church or a class in school, you can soon see that some exercise leadership over others.

I have a younger sister and, when we were children, I would take the lead. I would decide what to play, where to go. When I was in primary school I was passionate about drama, and I vividly remember getting my five-year-old sister dressed up as an angel, standing her on the lounge windowsill and giving her a Bible to read. When I was about seven, I was given a glove puppet and I persuaded my teacher to let me organize a glove puppet Teddy Bears' Picnic performance. When I was nine, I took a script of Cinderella to school and persuaded my class to take it on. I was exercising influence. Everyone is a leader in this sense, whether to a greater or a lesser degree.

Leadership as position

If everyone has influence, fewer people hold positions of leadership. At school we might be a class representative or even head boy or girl. As adults we might lead a house group or music group in church; we might be a school head of department or manager of a medical practice, or a business manager with a large team to lead. All these are leadership positions and we are a leader by virtue of our position.

Having a leadership position can provide a great opportunity to learn to lead. Many church leaders look back to formative experiences leading Christian Unions at school or youth groups at church, or being a junior leader on a Christian camp. When I used to help run Christian camps for 12- to 15-year-olds, I remember that several of the teenagers started Christian groups back at their schools. It was an excellent way to learn to be a leader. At a recent conference, where we were exploring how to develop leaders, one minister recalled how, as a 17-year-old, he'd led a school Christian Union of a couple of hundred boys. Having shown some promise and been given a leadership position, he had become a leader.

Sometimes people are given leadership positions when they are not really leaders, however. Having a leadership position does not make someone a leader: a person may be a churchwarden simply because he is conscientious and hardworking, for example. This is where those who choose or elect leaders have to exercise discernment to ensure that the right people are in the right leadership positions.

And who are the 'right' people? Those who have leadership ability, and, in a Christian context, those who are gifted for and called to leadership.

Leadership as ability

The next aspect of leadership is ability. Ability is made up of several things: skill, knowledge and talent (which anyone may have) and a spiritual gift, which Christians may be given by God.

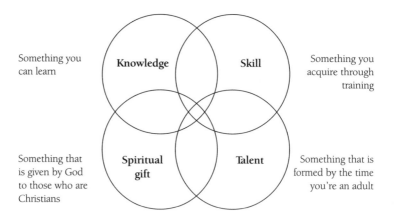

Something you can learn — **Knowledge** — **Skill** — Something you acquire through training

Something that is given by God to those who are Christians — **Spiritual gift** — **Talent** — Something that is formed by the time you're an adult

Skill

A skill is something you acquire through training—for example, how to set a good agenda, use a microphone, or run a computer software programme. Generally speaking, skills are transferable from one setting to another: the skill of setting good agendas can be transferred from a business context to a church or voluntary organization—although aspects of how the skill is applied may differ in each case.

Knowledge

Knowledge is something you can learn, gain more information about. For example, a newly appointed church leader will need knowledge about who does what in the church, the history of the church, and statistics about the local community. Leaders will bring many skills that are transferable from their previous context, but will need some fresh knowledge. They may also have acquired knowledge about how to understand the social dynamics of a community, and this can be transferred to the new situation.

Talent

The technical definition of talent is 'a recurring pattern of thought, feeling or behaviour that can be productively applied',[4] or, more simply, it is not what you *can* do but what you *can't help yourself doing*. Natural talents are often most obvious in the arts: for many people who can make music, draw or paint, it seems to come naturally; they can't help themselves doing it. Some people have a natural aptitude to lead. They can't help themselves doing it. In a group of people, they will take the initiative to get a task done and others will automatically look to them.

In the 1990s the Gallup organization researched thousands of leaders. This resulted in identifying the talents needed by leaders, which fall into four areas:

- Focus on the future: clarifying purpose and direction.
- Energy and drive: taking charge, doing something.
- Leading people: building relationships.
- Day-to-day delivery: creating the processes that make things happen effectively.

There are 20 'themes' that fall under these four headings, but no one leader has all 20. This is why leaders are so varied: there is no blueprint but a huge number of ways in which every leader may have some of those 20 themes in different combinations. These 20 are among the total of 34 themes of talent which have been recognized from Gallup's research. Talents can be identified through self-awareness, or through using a tool such as StrengthsFinder.[5]

One important thing about talents is that they develop in childhood and early adulthood, and are more or less formed by the late teens to early 20s. So the experiences of childhood and the teenage years are crucial in developing leadership talent—or any other kind of talent. It is possible to develop talents later, but it takes greater determination and persistence.

If natural talents are then developed with practice and honed with skills and knowledge, they become 'strengths'. A strength is not simply what we do well, but what gives strength to us. And the converse, weakness, is not necessarily something we are poor at but something that weakens us, drains us. Thus it makes sense to build on our strengths and find ways of compensating for our weaknesses—by not doing things we're not good at, by delegating to someone else or resigning ourselves to doing the best we can and getting a little better.

This exploration of leadership partly answers the age-old question of whether leaders are born or made. The answer is, not surprisingly, both! Some aspects of talent may well be inherited; then, early experiences of leadership contribute to producing leadership talent, which is then supplemented by hard work to acquire skills and knowledge.

Spiritual gift

Anyone can have skills, knowledge and talents for leadership, but only Christians can be given the spiritual gift of leadership. In most people there is a strong overlap between natural talent and spiritual gift, and it may be hard to distinguish between them.

In Romans 12:8, Paul refers to 'leading' as a gift. He writes, 'if [your gift] is to lead, do it diligently'; the Greek word used can mean 'to lead' or 'to care for', and the presence of this gift in a list of spiritual gifts implies that it is not intended to apply only to those who are leaders of churches. Then, as now, leaders are needed at all levels of church life, and leadership is a role, not an 'office' (such as deacon or presbyter).

According to the Bible, the responsibility of leaders is to prepare and equip the body of Christ for works of ministry. The New Testament picture of the body of Christ is of people all being gifted and called to serve in different ways. Some are called to lead. Those whom God chooses then have a responsibility to 'lead with diligence'. Diligence means constant or persistent endeavour, careful attention. One aim of this book is to help women who are called to lead to do so with diligence.

One important implication of leadership as a gift is that it is sometimes given to the most unlikely people. Think of someone like Gladys Aylward, who was turned down for missionary service but went to China anyway, and spread the gospel and led the movement for unbinding women's feet. In 1940, in order to evade capture by the Japanese, she led a group of 100 children over the mountains to safety. The gift of leadership is not a reward for long service; it's a tool for the job.

Leadership as call

Finally, the call to lead is as unique to Judeo-Christian leadership as is the idea of leadership as spiritual gift. Think of the call to Moses at the burning bush (Exodus 3) or to Jeremiah (Jeremiah 1). God calls people to leadership—and again, since this is God's choice, those chosen to lead are not always the ones we would choose or the ones who think themselves to be leaders. When I was exploring whether God was calling me to public ministry, as someone who struggled with speaking in public I found the story of Moses a great encouragement.

The assurance that we are called to lead is often what keeps us going when leadership seems to be a thankless task, when it requires hard decisions, when we are misunderstood, when we feel isolated. Many leadership roles in the Church are hard and demanding, and we may think, 'Who would want to do that?' In one sense, that is the wrong question. Those who want to fulfil those roles may be the wrong people. As the Anglican Church struggles to make sure it has a good process for choosing bishops, there is something to be said for not having an 'application' process. There is a sense in which we want as leaders those who accept the call but feel themselves to be unworthy servants, confident that the one who calls will also equip.

Most people exercise influence over others of one kind or another, only some have leadership positions, and fewer still have leadership ability. Those whom we think of as leaders normally have all three, and Christian leaders should be both gifted and called to lead. As Chapter 3 showed, however, women who have felt called to Christian leadership have often found their call unrecognized and been denied leadership positions. Some women, especially those from 'holiness' or charismatic backgrounds, have been accepted as leaders on the basis of their unequivocal call alone, while others have led by their influence, outside the structures of formal church 'position'.

DEFINING LEADERSHIP

The English word 'lead' comes from an Old English word *laedan*, meaning 'to take with one', 'to travel together to a new place'. So much for the word. Most modern definitions of leadership contain the three key concepts of going somewhere (*direction*), with an end in mind (*goal*) and taking *people* with you, either physically or metaphorically.

Steven Croft reminds us that 'the Judeo-Christian tradition

provides the longest continuous source of reflection on questions of leadership in the whole of human history'.[6] The Old Testament has a great deal to say, and the story of Moses has become a powerful prototype for leadership. While stories are told of good and less good leadership, a picture is built up of what makes effective leadership for the people of God. It is leadership that 'faces in two directions: the right and healthy ordering of the community and the relationship of that community to its wider environment'.[7] And at the heart of the portrait of good leadership are the words Samuel speaks to David at his anointing: 'The Lord does not see as mortals see; they look on the outward appearance, but the Lord looks on the heart' (1 Samuel 17:7, NRSV).

Many strands of leadership then flow into the portrait of Jesus in the Gospels, where Jesus is seen as king, prophet, priest and wisdom teacher. As Croft emphasizes, 'all subsequent reflection about church leadership needs to be informed by and measured against the pattern set by Jesus himself'.[8] Jesus exhibited humility and service, which are at the heart of leadership for Christians; he showed what it means to suffer in leadership; and, through the shape of his life, he influenced how others should lead.

Subsequent key strands of influence include writings by Gregory of Nazianzus, John Chrysostom and Pope Gregory the Great, the last of these focusing in particular on humility and pride. The Rule of St Benedict has also been influential, especially on religious communities. Among later writings are George Herbert's *The Country Parson* (1652) and Richard Baxter's *The Reformed Pastor* (1656), which focuses on leaders' oversight of themselves and of their flock. Among the best of the most recent writings, Croft chooses Walter Wright's *Relational Leadership* (2000) and Bill Hybels' *Courageous Leadership* (2002), which are rooted in scripture and full of profound leadership wisdom.

Defining Christian leadership

The definition used here was developed for the Arrow Leadership Programme, and is also used in *Growing Leaders*, the course for leaders at all levels in churches:

Christian leadership is
a servant-oriented relational process,
whereby those who lead, under God's leadership,
using their God-given capacity,
seek to influence others towards a kingdom-honouring goal.[9]

This definition highlights the fact that as Christian leaders our model is Jesus, the leader who taught his followers about leadership by washing their feet. The word 'relational' picks up on recent thinking about leadership and emphasis on its relational component. Leaders cannot afford to be entirely, or even primarily, task-focused, when leadership is about leading *people* to accomplish a task.

This definition focuses on leadership rather than 'a leader', and the use of the word 'those' highlights the corporate nature of leadership. In the New Testament, leadership was corporate, and this is fundamental to Christian leadership. In the 1980s, perhaps in reaction to too many autocratic leaders, there was a fashion for non-leadership, or 'facilitating'. At its best, a facilitator was a good democratic leader who involved others in leadership. At its worst, people sat around in a group, with everyone anxious not to take the initiative and 'lead' in case they upset anyone else. But the solution to bad leadership is not no leadership; it is good leadership.

The next clauses emphasize that all Christian leadership is under-leadership. People sometimes say, 'If you want to know if someone is a leader, look to see if anyone is following.' But for a Christian, this won't do. A Christian leader is first and foremost someone who is following Jesus. Henri Nouwen writes:

It is not enough for the priests and ministers of the future to be moral people, well trained, eager to help their fellow humans, and able to respond creatively to the burning issues of their time. All of that is very valuable and important, but it is not the heart of Christian leadership. The central question is, Are the leaders of the future truly men and women of God, people with an ardent desire to dwell in God's presence, to listen to God's voice, to look at God's beauty, to touch God's incarnate Word and to taste fully God's infinite goodness?[10]

We have already explored gifts, talents and ability. Leaders are people who acknowledge that their gifts and talents come from God, and seek to use them for the work of God.

The final part of the Arrow definition makes the point that leadership is about going somewhere. As someone has put it, leadership is not about taking a walk in the park. It is about influencing people towards a goal. And not just any goal, not a goal of the leader's own devising or one that serves their own agenda, but one that serves God's kingdom.

Leadership and charisma

Charisma is notoriously difficult to define. The word comes from the Greek, meaning 'gift' (hence the theological word 'charismatic'). 'Charisma' is usually used to imply a certain quality of personality, including a kind of personal magnetism, often coupled with persuasiveness and an uncanny ability to lead, charm, inspire and influence people. To some extent, all leaders have an element of charisma: being animated, listening and responding to others, connecting on an emotional level and using one's gifts to capture attention are useful attributes for leaders to have.

For many Christians, the leaders who inspire are 'charismatic', larger-than-life characters, who appear on platforms at conferences. But, interestingly, a piece of secular research has shown that it's not these 'larger-than-life' leaders who are the most effective. One of the most fascinating leadership books of recent years is *Good to Great*, a business book written by Jim Collins in 2001. Collins' aim was to try to establish what made a good company into a great company, and one of his key findings was that larger-than-life celebrity leaders were negatively correlated with taking a company from good to great. What the research found, somewhat surprisingly, was that the leaders who took companies from good to great were the opposite of the big personalities who are often thought of as great leaders.

Collins categorized leadership into five levels, the 'level 4' leader being the one often held to epitomize leadership. Like King David, the 'level 4' leader is the one who brooks no rivals and drives forward by force of his personality (and it usually is a 'him'), but Collins found that the most effective leaders were 'level 5 leaders' and precisely the opposite: 'Self-effacing, quiet, reserved, even shy, these leaders are a paradoxical blend of personal humility, and professional will, they are more like Lincoln and Socrates than Patton or Caesar.'[11] This cuts against the grain of conventional wisdom, especially the belief that leaders need to be hero figures with big personalities.

What is particularly significant about level 5 leaders from a Christian point of view is that they are not ambitious for themselves but are committed to a cause that is larger than themselves. They want to see their company (or organization) even more successful in the next generation. Christian leaders, too, ideally take the long view—although, sadly, I meet some who see leadership as power and want to be seen to be leading the largest and most successful church. Level 5 leaders also have intense professional resolve and take action. They are not the best leaders by accident. They work hard, make sacrifices and get the job done.

The other thing to note is that level 5 leaders look out of the window to apportion credit to factors outside themselves when things go well, but look at the mirror to apportion responsibility, never blaming bad luck, when things go poorly. Dame Marjorie Scardino, who in 1997 was appointed CEO of the global media empire Pearson plc, seems to illustrate this insight of Collins. When she worked for *The Economist* in New York, the circulation trebled under her leadership. Her perspective, however, was: 'The circulation grew a lot and everybody attributes that to me. But it was due to a group of people who knew what they were doing. The only smart thing I did was keep them on. They were the ones that did it, and I made sure they had food and water.'[12]

New directions for leadership

Leadership writer Peter Senge has written, 'In the knowledge era, we will finally have to surrender the myth of leaders as isolated heroes commanding their organizations from on high... Leadership in the future will be distributed among diverse individuals and teams who share responsibility for creating the organization's future.'[13]

Leadership is changing. Old dualistic and hierarchical models are disappearing in favour of egalitarian and holistic ones. The trend is towards leadership as team, and the idea that a leader is more like the conductor of an orchestra than the commander of an army. Leadership is shared rather than being the sole responsibility of one person.

In an article entitled 'Dorothy on Leadership', Brian McLaren has challenged traditional assumptions of leadership and, reflecting on the film *The Wizard of Oz*, suggests that the new leader is more like Dorothy than like the great Wizard—the imposing leader who is shown up at the end of the film to be a sham, an ordinary man hiding behind a curtain. Dorothy does not have all the answers but she draws in others to help her in her quest.[14] In a similar way, old film heroes like Superman and the Lone Ranger are being replaced by Frodo, Aragorn and Neo, self-questioning people who rely on those around them. In Peter Jackson's film *The Fellowship of the Ring,* Frodo says, 'I will carry the Ring to Mordor... though I do not know the way.'

Others have drawn new insights from the 'new science'—that relationships, not lone individuals, are the basic organizing unit of life; that chaos and change are inevitable and can be positive; that participation and cooperation are essential in this interconnected world.[15] 'What if leadership has more to do with finding meaning than in setting direction?' asks Leonard Hjalmarson.[16] This assumes that people are already going somewhere but need leadership to make sense of the journey rather than to motivate them to act. And if leadership is corporate rather than individual, then leadership may be a process in which an entire community is engaged, rather than something a leader does 'to' or 'for' another group of people. In our postmodern context, leadership is being redefined.

These new directions are significant to bear in mind as we come to look at women and leadership. Where do women fit into this new image of leadership?

WOMEN AND LEADERSHIP

Some women look at leaders of the 'great man' type, and think, 'I'm not like that, so I'm not a leader, and I could never be a leader.' Some look at behaviourist, task-oriented models and think, 'I don't feel comfortable giving orders or instructions.' Many women have rejected these and other traditional models of leadership; and, because these have been prevailing models and women have often not fitted them, both men and women have at times seen 'woman leader' as an oxymoron. Now leadership is being further reconfigured—more quickly in a secular context than in the Church but, remarkably, in ways that are more true to Jesus than much 'Christian leadership' has been. I used to have on my shelves a book called *All Truth is God's Truth*, and I find it both exciting that others are discovering God's truth when it comes to leadership and sad that sometimes Christians are the last people to see that it is happening.

New insights and models

In 1990 Judy Rosener, a leading researcher into leadership, published a paper entitled 'Ways women lead' in the *Harvard Business Review*. Rosener found that the way women led corresponded with the 'transformational' style of leadership. On the other hand, men were more likely to describe themselves in ways that corresponded with the older 'transactional' model. Men tended to rely on formal position and authority, and to achieve goals through reward and punishment. Women depended on their personality and used interpersonal skills to inspire and stimulate their followers or employees, in order to achieve their goals.

While these findings were initially challenged, they were confirmed in further studies. And while, in the 1960s and '70s, women commonly minimized the differences between men and women because those differences worked mainly to women's disadvantage, the tide seems to have turned. Now that the transformational style of leadership, the style most favoured by women leaders, is acknowledged to be more effective, it becomes easier for women to own this difference—without saying that the style is unique to women.

Christian thinking on women leaders

As attention has been focused on women as leaders, some writers have been exploring new images and models that embody some of the gifts women may bring to leadership. Jeanne Porter, in her book *Leading Ladies*, presents four images of leadership that contrast with the more male images of 'director', 'captain', 'commander' and 'helmsman'. The leader as 'midwife' is one who helps to bring to birth ideas and dreams, helping people to realize their God-given potential. The leader as 'choreographer' brings together the dance steps of individuals into 'a graceful movement of collective purpose'.

The leader as 'weaver' sees the future and weaves strands of people together to create something beautiful. The leader as 'intercessor' speaks for those who have no voice in order to bring about their freedom.[17] There is a rich variety of patterns and models waiting to be discovered.

Other women have reflected on the challenges and opportunities of leadership for Christian women today. One such woman is Roberta Hestenes, who has held a variety of leadership positions in universities and Christian organizations in the USA. In a paper published in 2006[18] she ponders some of the challenges: a combative environment, where the whole concept of women leaders is attacked (which is bound to make it harder to be a leader); the 'tall poppy syndrome', where anyone aspiring to a leadership role is seen as arrogant and cut down; the diffusion of power and authority, sometimes rightly as Christians use their gifts (which means that in some contexts anyone can do what leaders do); and the demands of leadership, which are higher than ever.

How do women lead? Do women lead differently? The next chapter explores in more detail the history of 'difference', how it has affected women as leaders in the past and its implications for the leadership of the future.

QUESTIONS FOR REFLECTION AND DISCUSSION

- Who or what comes to mind when you think about the word 'leader'? Why do you think this is?
- How have you had influence as a leader? What positions of leadership have you had? Reflect on any occasions where you have had significant influence without being in a formal leadership position.
- How do you understand the balance between leaders being 'born' and being 'made'?

✛

Chapter 5

DO WOMEN LEAD DIFFERENTLY?

'HE is confident; SHE is conceited
HE stands firm; SHE is hard
HE exercises authority; SHE is power mad
HE is close-mouthed; SHE is secretive.'
ANON

We learn at a very young age that there are two kinds of people: male and female. Infants as young as nine months can tell the difference between male and female faces. From an early age, we subconsciously learn who we are in relation to our gender.

What do those differences mean? Are men and women really so different? Do women and men act differently, behave differently, lead differently? And if they do, are the differences due to some innate quality or is it all down to individual personality?

The question of difference is central to the issue of women as leaders, since, as we have seen, some Christians argue that the differences between men and women are part of God's design for humankind, such that men are designed to lead and women not to lead.

It is also important because of its emotional effect on women. Women who are raised in the evangelical tradition, especially in churches where women's leadership is questioned, find it hard to get away from the internalized question, 'Should you really be doing this?' This question may seem particularly acute when women feel under pressure. Is there something about women that makes them less fitted, less well equipped for leadership? And when it comes to the question of senior posts in the Church, should women aspire to all roles or be confined (for example) to those that do not entail overall leadership? Thus the issue of difference affects women leaders in the Church in a variety of ways.

In the last 30 years or so, the arguments around sex-based difference have ranged to and fro, from, at one extreme, those who think that men and women are 'simply the same thing with different fittings' to those who argue that there is a patriarchal bias in humanity, essential differences between men and women beyond the obvious biological ones, such that men and women are destined for different kinds of lives: different roles in the family, in society and in the Church. In other words, are differences 'hard-wired', biologically and genetically determined, more than they are socially constructed?

In the midst of competing claims, fiercely argued, how are we to find the truth? And what implications does it have?

GENDER STEREOTYPES

'Men are from Mars, women are from Venus'?

Most people are familiar with the idea of differences between men and women. To give a few examples:

- Women are better than men at dealing with emotions.
- Men are better at taking risks.
- Women are more likely to follow instructions and ask for help.
- Men are better than women at reading maps.

But if we think about such stereotypes more closely, we know that, while there is some truth in them, there are also many exceptions. We know men (such as my husband) who are better than many women at dealing with emotions and women (such as myself) who are good at reading maps. If we look at scripture, Jesus was remarkably free from the stereotypes of our day, and certainly of his.

He welcomed children, cooked a meal on the beach, suffered pain without complaint and instructed people to turn the other cheek rather than fighting back.

One of the reasons why 'difference' has become so contentious is that certain differences have been used as reasons why men and women should or should not have particular roles in society.

Women are supposed to be 'more emotional' than men, and this has often been used as an argument for women not doing things (being leaders, managers, priests…), because the 'right' way to do things (according to men) is to make logical and rational decisions. If it were the case that being in touch with your emotions was a positive quality—as the concept of 'emotional intelligence' suggests—then for women to be 'more emotional', more in touch with feelings, might well equip them to be *better* leaders, decision makers, or whatever is the point at issue.

Of course, a prior question will be, 'Are all women more emotional than all men—or are such differences conditioned by upbringing, expectation and experience?' Logic has been admired as a quality in men, so men have been taught not to show their feelings or to cry. Women, on the other hand, have always been expected and encouraged to show their emotions and, by repeated experience, it has become 'natural'.

Views that rest on an assumption of biological determinism are suspect because there is no clear evidence of any behavioural trait being uniquely determined by biology. In addition, determinist views are problematic for Christians: if people are simply victims of their genes or hormones, then where is personal responsibility, and where is the place for repentance and acting differently?

Difference: a brief history

Knowledge is not value-free. It is constructed and, to some extent, historically relative. Hence we need a historical perspective to see how current views about male–female differences have been constructed through history.

Women were first described as chattels, as possessions of men, in the law codes of ancient Babylon, in about 1750BC. In the poetry of Homer, which laid the foundation of belief for Greek society, women were the source of conflict and suffering, even though they played no active roles. The philosopher Plato (c.429–347BC) declared females inferior in goodness to males, while his pupil Aristotle wrote that a female was a deformed male.

Christianity was born into a culture in which the roles of men and women were clearly defined. As we have seen, religious life in Old Testament times was structured such that only men were kings, priests and prophets, but there were exceptions. At the time of Christ, men had public roles while women were largely confined to the household. There was nothing 'Christian' about this; it was a feature of Greco-Roman society. But things were beginning to change and, in some cultural settings, women were beginning to have more freedom.

While society was seeing changes, Jesus seems to have gone even beyond these. Women, who had been prevented from playing a full part in the religious life, were able with him to do so. Mary sat at Jesus' feet not only to learn but as a potential teacher. One of the attractions of Jesus' teaching for women then (as well as more recently in places like Africa and India) was the new role and status they were granted in the Christian community. While slavery continued, and women were still theoretically subject to the household codes, the seeds of equality in Christ were sown.

As time went by and Christianity came under increasing threat from Rome, it seems that the Church made more concessions to the patriarchal culture and women began to take a lesser place. While some early Church writers took a more enlightened view of women, more commonly dualist notions from Greek philosophy affected attitudes to women: female nature was flawed and thus women were disqualified from leadership. This attitude permeated Christianity for a long time and, to some extent, does so today. Some of the arguments still being used in the 1980s and early 1990s against women being ordained to the priesthood, or against women being leaders in independent churches, were based on the idea that they are more gullible, more emotional and sources of sexual temptation to men. I can still remember telling my car mechanic, who was an elder in a free church, that I was going off to college to prepare to be ordained. 'I'm afraid I don't believe women should be leaders,' he said. 'Genesis 3: Eve was deceived by the serpent—women are much too gullible to be leaders!'

'He for God only, she for God in him' (Milton)

Until the 18th century there was a strong belief in the 'great chain of being' that had God at the top, then man, then woman, then animals, birds and so on, down to minerals of the earth. This idea goes back to Aristotle, the Greek philosopher of the fourth century BC, and was promoted by the Church; implicit was the idea that man was closer to God than woman was, because she was closer to sinful nature. Interestingly, as these ideas took root in European thought, it became only *European* man who was closest to God; other races were slotted in between Europeans and animals, a view to be challenged only 200 years ago as part of the rethinking of slavery.

Curious views about women distorted perceptions further. Before the Middle Ages, women's disturbing variability of mood was attributed to the movement of the womb around the body. The closer it moved to the head, the more likely it was to disturb behaviour. Then, in the Middle Ages, when detailed dissection began, it was seen that the womb does not move! An alternative explanation was needed.

But the womb—the most obvious symbol of women's difference from men—continued to be the focus of explanations about women. During the 19th century it was held up as a prime reason both for restricting education for women and for not giving women the vote.

The general notion was that the body only had a limited amount of energy and, in woman, the demands of childbearing meant that there was little left for other activities. If women overexercised their brains, it might do irreparable damage to their reproductive systems and they would not be able to exercise their 'rightful' role as mothers. The uterus or the ovaries were portrayed as dominating the entire personality of women.

These pronouncements about the damage women would experience expanded around the time that pressure was building up to allow women into higher education. Women who did struggle to enter higher education were viewed with contempt and scorn, and they were warned that the 'mental woman' was liable to become muscular and masculine, a monstrous production. This is just one example of how knowledge can be historically determined, and shows how views on 'difference' are far from being factual. In 1913, a book argued against female suffrage on the grounds that women were incapable of the rational capacity needed to decide how to vote.

To some extent these views still linger. Being seen as an 'intelligent woman' can sometimes mean being viewed as something of an aberration. At school, girls over a certain age may be wary of competing with their peers and appearing 'clever'. Yet people rarely say that about men. We may lament the lack of women with PhDs in theology, or teaching in theological colleges, but it can still be harder for women than for men to embark on an academic career.

Of course, the view that work and thought would damage women only applied to middle-class women. Working-class women were expected to do manual work, and the arguments about fertility did not seem to matter in their case.

Separate spheres

In the 19th century another dynamic was at work, the notion that men and women operated in separate spheres, each with different powers.

The woman's sphere was essentially the private one, removed from the public world of men. This view arose in Britain as society changed from a pre-industrial to an industrial one. The differences between women and men intensified as men went 'out to work', running factories or working in offices; and men aspired to demonstrate their position in society by having a wife at home who did not work but who looked after children and the domestic sphere. This view that men were designed for the public and women for the private, home world still persists in some cultures and religious traditions today.

But once women began to enter the workforce and earn their own money, the tide started to turn. World wars drew them into the workforce in unprecedented numbers, and, while they were to some extent not needed afterwards, it was more difficult to argue that they could not do the jobs they had been doing. In the post-war years, a new version of the middle-class stay-at-home housewife emerged, but, when more and more women had tasted a new freedom, the time was ripe for a new assertion of women's rights, and the 'women's liberation movement' was born.

Gender differences had been used to women's disadvantage as many so-called 'feminine' traits were valued negatively: women were seen as submissive, lacking in independence, indecisive and so on. Thus 1960s feminism aimed to minimize differences. If men and women were much the same, then women could be admitted to professions, occupations, sports and activities that were previously open only to men.

Since then, arguments have become more nuanced. Current research seems to suggest that biology is relevant, but that it is meaningless to separate it out from other aspects of human development. To give one example, Simon Baron-Cohen's book *The Essential Difference* (2004) makes the case that the female brain is predominantly hardwired for empathy, while the male brain is hardwired for building and understanding systems. However, such differences are not due entirely to biological factors but also to social ones, and Baron-Cohen is careful to talk about the diversity that is found within genders, and to point out that looking for sex differences is not the same as stereotyping men and women.

God and gender difference

In an influential book published in 1973, *The Inevitability of Patriarchy*, Steven Goldberg concluded that all societies have been patriarchal and always will be. It is true that most societies have been male-dominated but, as Christians, we do not take what has been, in a fallen world, as determinative of what should be in a redeemed world. If patriarchy is one result of the Fall, we would expect to find that most or all societies have been patriarchal, but this does not tell us that they should be. As Christians our reference point must be the Bible, correctly interpreted.

Genesis tells us that God created human beings male and female. Why God decided to create two similar but different kinds of most creatures is a mystery, but the fact is that he did, and these two entities appear to be linked to his image: 'So God created human beings in his own image, in the image of God he created them; male and female he created them' (Genesis 1:27). Gender is deliberate. Man is not the image of God by himself; woman is not the image of God by herself. The two genders together help us to see what God is like, and men and women are much more alike than they are different.

Reflecting on the character of God, as he is portrayed in scripture, may reveal more about so-called male and female characteristics. God values relationships, something often associated with women. God sent us his Son in order to restore our relationship with him. Valuing relationships is not a woman-thing, it is a God-thing, and thus something that both women and men should value. Leadership and strategy are also part of who God is. God chose Moses to bring his people out of slavery to freedom and led them in the desert with a pillar of smoke by day and fire by night. God sent prophets to remind people of who they were and of who he was; he devised a plan to save us when we could not save ourselves. Leading and strategizing reflect who God is, and thus should be important to both men and women.

So it might be with a number of characteristics that are often categorized as 'masculine' or 'feminine'. I have often reflected on the fruit of the Spirit (Galatians 5:22–23) and wondered whether some of the men who expound this passage actually think gentleness is a fruit that they should produce, just as they would expect it of women. Or self-control—how often I have heard it said that men cannot be expected to 'control themselves': a man has to be a man.

HOW DO WOMEN LEAD?

Research on leadership and difference

Leadership and difference has been the subject of research in women's leadership and management studies for the past 30 years. In a paper published in 1987,[1] Susan Vinnicombe reported that women and men showed different styles of leadership. Out of five managerial styles, the majority of men were 'traditionalists', followed by 'visionaries'. Only 25 per cent of the women were 'traditionalists', with the majority being 'visionaries', followed by 'catalysts'. (Visionaries are supposed to be 'natural' strategic leaders and excel if given free rein, but may rebel if they feel constrained.) This pattern fits in with perceptions of women leaders 20 or 30 years ago as sometimes being critical of their organization, too independent and poor with systems and routines.

Other studies from around this time tended to be conflicting, some showing men's styles to be more competitive, controlling and hierarchical, with women's more collaborative and cooperative. On the other hand, some studies showed no consistent sex differences in leadership styles. Research by Alice Eagly and Blair Johnson published in 1990 concluded that the strongest evidence for difference in style was that women adopted a more democratic or participative style, and men a more autocratic or directive style. Men tended to be more task-oriented and women more interpersonally-oriented.[2]

The 1990s saw the acceleration of research on women and difference in leadership. 1990 also saw the publication of Judy Rosener's study, 'Ways women lead'. Rosener found that, while the first women executives had followed the leadership styles of men, a second wave of women were adopting new styles, drawing on skills and attributes they developed from their shared experience as women. They were succeeding not despite but because of certain characteristics considered to be 'feminine'.

A book published in 1990, *The Female Advantage: Women's Ways of Leading* by Sally Helgesen, took this argument a step forward. The book is based on the diaries of women leaders and seeks to share what they have to offer organizations in terms of leadership. Helgesen notes that, when women first entered the 'men's world' of leadership, they had to adopt strategies to lead like men did, in order to be accepted. As time went on, organizations started to become less hierarchical and, as a result, women were able to transform the workplace not by being something they were not but by being who they were.

Helgesen noted that, in a whole variety of ways, women led differently—not identifying themselves solely with their jobs as men often did, making time for networks of relationships outside the organizations, sharing information rather than keeping it to themselves. The prime difference was that men's work and personal lives were separate, while women did not separate themselves off in this way. She gave the example of an executive director who took her baby to the office when she worked on Sundays: '"Having a baby around... helps loosen these guys up, makes them more responsive. And it sends a message that we think the *whole* person is valuable around here."'[3]

Leading from the centre

Helgesen's subsequent book, *The Web of Inclusion* (1995), continued the conversation, exploring how women leaders prefer to work in flattened, interwoven organizational structures—webs of relationships. Through these webs, women maximize productivity and innovation. Women often refer to themselves as being in the middle of things—not at the top, but in the centre. This web image also influences such things as management structure and ways of structuring meetings. Web is perceived as directly opposed to hierarchy.

The first sex

This line of thinking was extended by Helen Fisher in her book *The First Sex: the Natural Talents of Women and How They Are Changing the World* (1999). To suggest that women have particular 'natural talents' appears to be reverting to stereotypes, but Fisher and others have been careful to suggest that such patterns of difference as they observe are not necessarily connected to any fixed or inherent biological differences between men and women. Fisher notes that each of us is a complex mixture of so-called masculine and feminine traits. We are influenced by hormones, which are also on a continuum. In addition, environmental forces take up the job of shaping who we are.

Fisher builds on the idea that women often bring different skills—'web' thinking, for example—and that, in a business context, women's skills and thinking are becoming more highly valued. There is some evidence to suggest that women are apt to think long-term more regularly, while men focus on the here and now. Women are more likely to be team players, wanting to share power. They are less comfortable in rigid hierarchical settings.

She argues that, while differences were used in the past to keep women in second place, things are different now. Women have demonstrated their ability and will move into 'changing the world'. The secret of this? Women born in the post-war baby boom are reaching middle age, and the menopause, a time when women often become more assertive, will have a significant impact on the next 20 years as older women step up into leadership. The higher levels of testosterone released at this time, relative to declining levels of oestrogen, have the effect of giving women increased confidence.

Fisher argues that in the future more parents will revel in 'It's a girl'. In the past—and, sadly, still today—in some societies people rejoiced in the birth of boys but baby girls were rejected. Now, by contrast, 'We are inching towards a truly collaborative society, a global culture in which the merits of both sexes are understood, valued and employed. The twenty-first century may be the first in the modern era to see the sexes work and live as equals—the way men and women were designed to live.'[4]

In a recent book, *Closing the Leadership Gap* (2004), Marie Wilson explores how society might change from a system built on the labour of women to one led equally by their vision. Her goal is to change the expectations of both sexes so that men and women can integrate the satisfactions of leadership and family life. This would involve organizations having more family-friendly policies, such as part-time working and gender-neutral flexitime. Over the last few years we have been seeing this begin to happen.

Are women clergy different?

As we come to look at leadership difference in the Church, one intriguing factor is that some research suggests that female (and male) church leaders are different from the norm. Research published in 1992 on male and female clergy in the Anglican Church[5] found that male clergy tended to exhibit personality characteristics commonly associated with feminine stereotypes, while female clergy exhibited stereotypically male characteristics. Women clergy were found to be more tough-minded, more extraverted and more outgoing than male clergy. It appears from more recent research that this may be due to the resilience needed by the first women ordained, who had to face a long battle before being ordained first deacon in 1987, and then priest in 1994.

There may also be differences in the personalities of those ordained at different stages of the deliberations about women priests in the Church of England. One interesting line of thought is that many of the women in ministry before 1992 (as deaconess or deacon) were, in Myers-Briggs terms, like clergy men—mainly NFPs (in other words, more 'feeling' than 'thinking'). In the first generation of women selected for priesthood after the 1992 vote, there were many whose preferences were NTJ—more 'thinking' in their preferences than the previous generation of women and than many of their male colleagues. Thus ordained women are not always 'typical' of women in general, whatever that means!

HOW DO WOMEN IN THE CHURCH LEAD?

There has been little research on differences between men's and women's leadership styles in the Church. A research project by Christian Research in 1997, using Christian Research Association members, found that male clergy were more likely to be 'directors' than women clergy, who were primarily team people.

Helen Thorne conducted a research project on the first women priests in the Church of England, published in 2000.[6] She found that those women had a collaborative leadership style, and suggested that the reason was that women had initially adopted collaborative working patterns in order to survive patriarchal structures in society and had found this way of working empowering. They thus brought a different, fresh approach to ordained ministry. Other women have reiterated this interpretation, that 'collaboration' is learned behaviour rather than 'natural' or 'innate'.[7] Those women who were in ministry for some years before they became priests had discovered the value of collaboration, since without a formal leadership position it is the only way to get things done. It is not yet clear, therefore, whether women are necessarily more collaborative than men or whether their role as assistants has tended to make them so.

As many men are now adopting a collaborative style, so it is becoming less obviously 'female'. I know both male and female ministers who have encountered opposition when trying to exercise this style. It can look like weakness to delegate, consult and try to empower others when you are taking over the job of a previous leader who was much more autocratic, and, if members of the congregation expect the authorized minister to do most of the work, much re-education is needed. In the Church, as in society, younger leaders of both sexes are likely to lead collaboratively, which will be expected by younger congregations but may prove harder to exercise among older ones.

Women church planters

In 1996 I carried out some research on women and church planting. Among other things, I was interested to see whether women approached church planting in the same way as men, or whether they led differently. The answers to this question were intriguing. Almost exactly half the women said they thought they led differently from the way a man would lead, and the other half said they thought men and women led in a similar way, any differences being the result of different personalities. When the responses were analysed, a pattern emerged. Some of the women had experience in raising families but little experience of paid work outside the Church. These were the women who thought they brought a 'woman's touch' to church planting, that they were more collaborative and nurturing, more pastoral in their approach than men might have been. Some of the other women had moved from executive posts—and it was these who believed that they did not lead differently because they were women. They brought leadership skills from the workplace rather than the home.

What this suggested was that women would bring to church leadership whatever transferable skills they already possessed. As women's and men's experiences and spheres were becoming more blurred, any perceived differences would probably become less marked.

Other comments from the women surveyed included the following:

- Many struggled with a sense of inferiority, and therefore needed extra assurance of God's will to meet the inevitable challenges. Several interpreted this as an area of spiritual attack.
- Some were used to having supportive roles and deferring to men, and therefore found it hard to step up to lead.
- Several felt there was a perception that the plant was a less valid church if led by a woman (though this may relate to the status of church plants as much as to perceptions of women leaders).
- One woman found that other women in the church were unable to hide in traditional women's roles (because she was a more collaborative, enabling leader), and some felt threatened by this.
- Another felt strongly that differences between men and women were few, and that we should expect more from both sexes. Satan has a vested interest in limiting what God can do through us all.

Women church leaders

'Women work through relationships; men work by being seen.' That was an instant comment on men and women as leaders made to me recently by one woman. A couple of years ago, I surveyed a number of women in church leadership, asking about leading differently. This time, almost all the women said that any differences in how they led were due to differences of personality, not gender:

'In the end I think it's more based on personality.'
'I think the main differences depend on the individual.'

However, most of them also qualified this with a 'But...' generalization about women. This was largely what I expected, but interesting nevertheless. They thought women:

- are less charismatic figures and tend to lead more quietly.
- lack confidence.
- are normally democratic, and have to learn to lead from the front when appropriate.
- are less motivated by power, status and ambition.
- are better at team building and delegating, and are more approachable than men.
- are better at multi-tasking and multi-viewing.
- are generally more collaborative.
- are better at reading people.
- are more concerned about pastoral issues.
- are quick to draw alongside people.

One woman suggested several possible differences but added, 'Having said that, I think that in most respects my own ministry is as different from other women's as it is from most men's.'[8] In other words, most women could think of ways in which their style differed from men's but did not want to push too far towards stereotypes and generalizations.

Rethinking leadership

In 2004 Molly Marshall was elected president of a Baptist seminary in the USA, the first woman to assume such a post. She has consciously sought to rethink leadership:

One of the things I've been trying to do is learn more, to ask the question, 'What constitutes effective leadership?' I try not to rely on patterns of the past... I am shaped by the Benedictine tradition of spirituality. One of the ideas of the Rule is that the leader should never do anything without counsel. This is something I regularly practice through consulting with board members, faculty, even students.[9]

Another challenge to traditional leadership is the concept of leading from the middle rather than from above. Alice Mathews argues for leadership 'from the middle, where leading enables people to address their problems satisfactorily... Leadership is the process of bringing people to the point of having to face their problems and to deal with them.'[10] Roberta Hestenes has explored three basic 'postures' of leadership: leading from below, from above and from the side She noted that in leading from above she was tempted to deny the power and influence she had; she found it hard to cope with the 'strong woman' image and wanted to soften it. As she settled into her leadership role, she adopted what she calls 'leading from the side', arguing that much of leadership is not about position but about people and networks, so it is about getting alongside people as individuals and in groups or meetings. The leader is then creating win–win situations, with the power inherent in leadership used to support and cooperate, not dominate.[11]

Hestenes also argues against clear difference between male and female styles—women differ from each other, as men do—and different contexts require different approaches. Her approach to how women lead is more nuanced, and she suggests that we cannot make simplistic generalizations when there are so many factors to be considered. Leaders' styles will relate to the context, their giftedness, skills and experience, and how they use the gifts God has given.

In her sabbatical study of women leaders in the Anglican Church, Elizabeth Dyke notes the following comments from women in senior posts in Canada and the UK:

There is a strong interplay of gender and social conditioning in how both men and women lead—it is not purely one or the other. Gender-related perceptions of behaviour can colour how leadership is experienced. A woman may be perceived as strident or aggressive whereas the same behaviour in a man is interpreted as strong and assertive.

Leadership style is more to do with personality than gender, but we have our understanding of leadership formed more by male role models, simply because there are more of them!

Leadership is about handling power and authority. Women are not always comfortable with power. They tend to operate more through collaboration and team than hero leadership or executive power.[12]

There are thus a variety of factors involved in how women choose to lead and how their leadership is perceived by others.

Reflecting on Christian leadership early in 2007, Sally Morgenthaler notes that, while the world has gone relational, the leadership default in many organizations (including church ministry) is still top-down, 'command and control'. In these organizations, the so-called 'soft' skills are seen as feminine and therefore weak, time-consuming, indecisive and manipulative. But these skills work in new companies such as Google—as we might expect. So Morgenthaler urges women in church leadership not to throw out their soft skills and upgrade to hard; they can use both. The best leaders take charge, they lead, but they are also organic about strategy, able to let go the reins of control and involve people's passions in the process.

Leading alongside

'Some of the best leaders don't know where they are going.' This was a saying used at a consultation on leadership in 1998. It may seem to contradict traditional notions of leadership but it echoes the thoughts of those who have perceived a shift to a different approach. Here the leader is someone who has the humility to understand that he or she can travel beyond the known into the anxiety of the unknown, taking others as fellow travellers who will sometimes follow and sometimes take a lead themselves.

When Lynn Cheyney was interviewed for the job of senior pastor in a large church in Chicago, she surprised the search committee by replying to their question, 'What would be your vision for the church?' 'I have no idea. I don't know you yet. Discerning the vision for the church is something we would do together.' She was the first candidate who had not said, 'Here's what we need to do!' and presented a programme.[13] Leadership has often been seen as being about the leader, like Moses, going 'up the mountain' to receive the vision from God. Today, however, leaders are encouraged to work with people and develop a vision together, on the basis that a shared vision will be owned by more people and a collaborative exercise will bring together more gifts and talents to make it a better process. This is a much more New Testament picture of how leadership is exercised.

Leaders who are secure can admit that they do not know where they are going. In this period of rapid change, fewer people admit to knowing what the answers are; sometimes we do not even fully understand the questions. As a number of writers have pointed out recently, leaders of the future will have to live with provisionality, risk, failure and experiment. What other options do we have?

At this time in the Church's history it is clear that many things are not clear! After a couple of decades of 'answers' to the problems of evangelism or church growth, we are now certain of one thing: there are no 'one size fits all' answers. A leader must sometimes be one who does not know where a particular church is going, but has the courage to help people to find out. This is much more healthy and empowering, drawing on the gifts of all the baptized, than the hierarchical command and control style, which draws on extra-biblical philosophical and military models.

Leading growing churches

In his book *The Road to Growth,* Bob Jackson communicates his research on why churches grow. In a chapter entitled 'Church growth through good practice' he presents evidence of attendance change in parishes with a woman incumbent. With a caveat about the relatively small number (75 parishes) over a short time period, he concludes, 'It does increasingly seem that women are, on average, leading growing churches and being rather more successful in this than men.'[14]

Jackson suggests several theories as to why this might be: that women of the first generation of priests have had to be exceptionally determined; that women have usually been given smaller or less well regarded livings, so they have found it easier to grow a church from a lower base; or that they are more naturally relational than men, which is more useful than policies or programmes in growing communities. Putting together several church growth factors, he suggests, 'The ideal candidate profile for a church that wishes to grow would appear to be young, female, and willing to stay in post for ten to twelve years!'[15]

As we've seen, women seem to be more collaborative leaders, and this is vital in a climate where there will be fewer full-time, paid church leaders and more teams and groups involving paid and unpaid, ordained and lay leaders. Women leaders are also paying attention to areas and issues that have previously been neglected in the Church, including areas often seen as 'women's issues', such as rape and domestic violence.

But if women, for whatever reason, bring to ministry the gifts needed for leadership in the future, and they have proved in many spheres of leadership to be as competent as men, this should surely be more widely recognized.

ENLIGHTENED POWER

The introduction to *Enlightened Power*, a collection of 40 articles by business and other entrepreneurial leaders on many aspects of women's leadership, says this:

Our resounding vision is one of organizations that invoke the full participation of men and women leaders... we are changing the nature and use of power through our use of enlightened power—that which is manifest as we enact inclusive leadership that brings to bear the full and equal partnership of men and women leaders.[16]

It would be wonderful if the Church, which has been entrusted with perhaps the fullest vision of this equal partnership, could show the way. As it is, in so far as we open up new possibilities for women's leadership in the Church, we have new opportunities to learn from those who have paved the way in other fields.

Here are a few examples of how women's gifts might enhance the Church today:

- **In our changing culture:** church decline figures speak for themselves, and the Church is perceived as increasingly out of touch with society. Women appear to bring long-range and strategic thinking, which will be needed as we address the future.
- **Challenges of finance and clergy/leadership deployment:** many denominations have responded by renewed emphasis on collaborative ministry, ministry leadership teams and so on, for which women appear to be gifted.
- **The need for unity in the face of division:** there is evidence that women use more democratic, inclusive and unifying strategies and could be a real key to unity, rather than—as is so often argued in the debate about women bishops, for example—a source of disunity.

In conclusion, while women, through most of church history, have been seen as 'different', inferior to men and incapable of leadership, such ideas have been disproved and exposed as relics of patriarchy and prejudice. In the professional world, women have proved themselves to be capable and effective leaders, and a number of gifts that many women possess seem to make them uniquely fitted for leadership in the Church today. It is time that women whom God has gifted for leadership had those gifts fully recognized, so that they are able to take their God-given place alongside men, in partnership in the gospel.

QUESTIONS FOR REFLECTION AND DISCUSSION

- How has the idea that men are the norm and women are 'different' affected your society and the lives of women around the world?
- How do you suppose men's and women's bodies affect the way they each think and behave?
- Do you think women lead differently from the way men lead? What have you observed in yourself and those you know?
- What is your vision for women in the Church?

—— Part 3 ——

ISSUES WOMEN FACE

While there may be few biologically based differences between men and women that affect their leadership, as relative newcomers to leadership and facing male styles and ways of doing things, women leaders face a number of issues. Chapter 6 explores the concepts of power, which many women find problematic, and service, which is key to Christian leadership but may tap into unhelpful patterns and expectations that women have inherited. Chapter 7 looks at two attributes of leadership, confidence and courage. Many women lack confidence and, as leaders, find that growing in confidence is a vital part of their development. Courage is often seen as the province of men but is vital to leadership, so the chapter looks at how women can own courage and grow in the kind of courage needed for leadership.

Chapter 8 focuses on a number of areas found to be key for the development of women as leaders, and explores two tools—mentoring and developing a life statement—that women can use to help them in their development. This chapter thus has a more practical feel. Following the Conclusion, there is a Resource Section.

✥

Chapter 6

POWER AND SERVICE

'When a woman responds to a call to ordination it is frequently seen as a failure to be content with a life of service and an inappropriate seeking after power; but when a man responds… it is called "responding to the call to serve".' [1]

Thinking about leadership can be confusing for women. As we have seen, collaborative and relational styles of leadership are coming to the fore in the business world and in parts of the Church, but past models of leadership on offer to women have not always seemed very attractive. While Christian leadership is supposed to be modelled on Jesus, attitudes of humility and service have not always been in evidence. We defined Christian leadership as 'a servant-oriented relational process', but often it has appeared to be the opposite—at its most extreme, motivated by desire for power, prestige and control rather than servant-like, motivated by love and enabling; hierarchical and solo rather than relational.

For most of the past 2000 years, church leadership has been dominated by men, so it is not surprising that some women associate leadership with male power. In most denominations, women have until recently been denied full participation in the life of the Church on the same basis as men. An invitation to join the male 'club', to sit at the top of the table or the top of the pyramid, therefore seems to some a rather mixed blessing. Women with gifts of leadership are delighted that at last they are able to use them. But sometimes, to become a leader seems like 'betrayal', changing sides to join the oppressor, and women are not always sure they want to do it when leadership is a costly enough business anyway. Some women find

138

themselves passive, giving power away in such a way that others use it over them, rather than being able to handle it well.

When women have answered the call to leadership, it has sometimes been perceived negatively by others as 'seeking power'. Because women's default mode has often been service, some have found it hard to step up to a position that feels unfamiliar and inevitably involves exercising authority and power. And with 'power and control' still a common model of leadership, women have found that to be accepted as leaders they have had to use this model while also trying to critique it.

No wonder some Christian women are ambivalent about leadership! This chapter explores these issues of power, authority, service and sacrifice as they affect women who are called to leadership, seeking to answer the following questions:

- In a church that has often been characterized by leadership as 'authority over', can women be themselves *and* lead in a collaborative and relational way?
- What does it mean for a woman positively to be a servant leader?
- How can leadership power be used rightly, to empower rather than to control?

RADICAL SACRIFICE

It is clear from the New Testament that Jesus found it difficult to convince even his closest followers that service was a valid model of leadership. There are traps in hierarchy: they attract the wrong people with the wrong motives, and Jesus was very clear that his way was different. He lived it, washing his disciples' feet. He taught it: 'You know that those who are regarded as rulers of the Gentiles lord it over them... Not so with you. Instead, whoever wants to become great among you must be your servant, and whoever wants to be first must be slave of all' (Mark 10:42–44). James and John had come with a request for the top places beside Jesus in glory. They had a lot to learn, but so do we all.

We do not know exactly what shape the table for the last supper was, but the inference is that it had no 'head', no top places, although some of the disciples were seated nearer to Jesus than others. And after that final supper, Jesus lived out his teaching. He died demonstrating in the most memorable way possible how to serve and sacrifice for the sake of others: 'For even the Son of Man did not come to be served, but to serve, and to give his life as a ransom for many' (v. 45).

Such is the power and pull of hierarchy that we have struggled to live out Jesus' radically countercultural teaching. We want to be 'on top'. We want to control things—and people. We want prestige, fame and adulation. We don't want to give that first place to God. But not giving him first place, not putting him at the centre of the Church—surely that is the essence of sin?

IDEAL V. REALITY

Two thousand years after Jesus taught us a new model of leadership, we still have not grasped it:

I seem to spend more time listening to laity struggling with outmoded ministerial leadership styles than to any other issue. Sadly, and perhaps surprisingly, it is evangelical churches where the problem seems to be most acute. Indeed the larger the church the larger the problem seems to loom… ministers are often working (unconsciously) on dated and dubious leadership models which are rooted in a past hierarchical culture. Such a leadership model sees the minister as responsible for providing the vision and direction, and for controlling the decision making processes, of the church. Under the guise of 'vision', 'leadership', 'gifting/ministry/anointing' pass such things as autocratic decision making, fear of delegation, fear of creativity, and fear of loss of control.[2]

Models of leadership drawn from the Old Testament have only limited application to the New. We have all heard sermons and read books about the leadership of people like Moses, Joshua, David and Nehemiah, but, while scripture describes, it does not always prescribe. Since Pentecost and the sending of the Spirit, the whole people of God have been given the Holy Spirit and are priests and kings. All have spiritual gifts and all have ministries.

John Adair notes that 'the problem for most leaders is that they have risen to their current position of power because of considerable ability and a dominant spirit, with the concept of being humble, of serving rather than ordering, proving difficult'.[3] People like this become leaders but find it hard to be like Jesus. Some might argue that many women would act with humility and a serving spirit—but, lacking encouragement and ambition, women less often attain those positions in order to demonstrate it!

Having a leadership position does not mean that a leader has to exercise 'positional leadership' (leading by virtue of their job title rather than their character or ability). Relational, collaborative leadership, in which a number of people are working together and using complementary gifts and strengths, will always be more effective—even if sometimes more difficult to achieve. No one leader has all the gifts and skills that are needed. It is increasingly recognized that the job of leader is to enable other people to exercise their ministry. The 'one-man band' is out—for more than one reason.

IN SEARCH OF A ROUND TABLE

One solution to leadership 'hierarchy', which is perceived negatively by many women, is the model of the 'round table', an image that derives from the table of King Arthur at Camelot, a utopian vision of community. This model has been explored by some feminist writers: women reject the idea of moving 'up' the table, and have envisioned the Church as a round table, which has no 'top' and 'bottom', but only equality.

A book was published in 1997 with the title *In Search of a Round Table: Gender, Theology and Church Leadership* (ed. Musimbi R.A. Kanyoro). Its contributors explore some of the conundrums of leadership, power and equality. If Christianity is about a discipleship of equals, how has it come to be so full of power, authority and privilege? Many women have perceived that it is no use just getting their place at the table. They also need to be involved in reshaping the table to accommodate their presence; otherwise, instead of women changing the structures, the structures may change women. A long, narrow table is detrimental to women, and to all who seek to be servant leaders.

A leadership structure of some kind is inevitable, however. There is a form of hierarchy in heaven: in the book of Revelation, John is shown a throne in heaven surrounded by 24 other thrones for the 24 elders (4:4). The disciples, rebuked by Jesus for squabbling about who is the greatest, are also told that 'when the Son of Man sits on his glorious throne, you who have followed me will also sit on twelve thrones, judging the twelve tribes of Israel' (Matthew 19:28).

Ultimately, it may not be the structure that is problematic, but the way it has been used. There will always be power and authority inherent in leadership. Men or women will be called to leadership positions. The question is how to lead from those positions in a way that does not domineer or exploit others. Hence the approach that speaks of leading differently, from the side or within. Such leaders have positional power but choose to share it with others in a way that is empowering.

THE LEADER AS SERVANT

The bowl and the towel

The classic biblical passage about leadership is John 13, where Jesus washes his disciples' feet. Jesus 'got up from the meal, took off his outer clothing, and wrapped a towel round his waist. After that, he poured water into a basin and began to wash his disciples' feet, drying them with the towel that was wrapped round him'(vv. 4–5).

Foot washing is mundane and basic, and it was the action of a slave. For Jesus to do it symbolized his laying aside of power, doing leadership differently. He did not come to be served but to serve. When we see a church leader (including the Archbishop of Canterbury) doing this on Maundy Thursday, we are struck by the juxtaposition of the supposed power and authority of leadership and this demonstration of the kind of leadership Jesus modelled. This action has become a sign of leadership: the sign of the bowl and the towel.

But what if the washer of feet is a woman?

Of course, the point is not whether or not we wash feet, but what we do that demonstrates the same kind of attitude: whether we will sit for hours with a frail old woman who is dying alone; whether we will spend hours with the difficult young man who is depressed and has lost the will to live; whether we will stay behind after the meeting to put the chairs away or do the washing-up.

Some of these actions are problematic for women because it is so often women who would do these things anyway—maybe not stacking the chairs, but the washing-up, the serving of refreshments, the clearing up in the kitchen, the hours of sitting and keeping company. Women often do these quiet and unspectacular things because that is what is expected, while some male church leaders seem only interested in doing the tasks where they will be seen and will soon make a name for themselves. I think of a male curate who decided quite early on that taking funerals would detract from the high-profile role he wanted, so he asked a licensed lay minister to do them.

Women's default mode?

If the Christian model is service, this can also be problematic for some women. While for men to act as servants is to make a significant countercultural gesture ('he's a great leader—he even does *those* things!'), women are used to serving others, including men, and putting others before themselves. Women have, in the past, been accustomed to serving refreshments, cooking meals, cleaning and housekeeping. The expectation that they will serve, rather than being able to choose freely to follow the example of Christ, can push women back into a service model. Evidence from one leadership programme that uses the word 'servant' suggests that some women find this uncomfortable, thinking that 'servant' is a 'male' idea. The term 'servant' is too closely associated with the more traditional role of women as providers for men. 'Service' can thus be more acceptable than 'position' for all the wrong reasons, and can become a cover for feelings of worthlessness

Jesus' service was freely chosen. For most women, service has not been chosen; it has been assumed and expected. Coming to a place where they too can make a free choice may entail a long journey, finding themselves before they can come to the point of giving themselves away again. If, for Jesus, taking the role of a servant was partly about giving power away, then perhaps women need to be encouraged first to discover who they really are before being helped to handle power rightly, in a way that enables others rather than disempowering them.

Embracing humility

The pagan world regarded humility as a vice rather than a virtue. That is another reason why Jesus was so misunderstood by some: his leadership was so countercultural. But when Jesus confronted his followers who were competing for status, he redefined greatness (Matthew 20:20–28), telling them that he had come to give his life 'for many'. Leaders will always be tempted to ask, 'What's in it for me?' but Jesus tries to show them another way, motivated not by a desire to be a martyr but by love for all people.

In the 19th century, humility was seen as a trait of the well-developed female, while pride and self-esteem became marks of mental health for men. While this is no longer the case, vestiges of it can be seen in the way, for example, that traits in a man that are seen as the exercise of authority may be seen in a woman as a sign of being power-mad. Many women have been anxious about this kind of labelling and reacted by denigrating themselves and their abilities. Thus it may be harder for women than for men to hear Christian teaching about humility in the right way. Jesus did not think too little of himself, yet many women have heard humility as meaning, 'Don't think about yourself, just think of others.' But when we think too little of ourselves, when we are afraid to be human, when we fail to accept our calling and refuse to celebrate our unique gifts and abilities, then we are far from being as God intends us to be.

What servant leadership is not

In some church traditions, Mary (the model of womanhood) is seen as passive, reinforcing the norm of women's general passivity and obedience to men. Seen from a different standpoint, however, Mary is a picture of active discipleship and visionary faith, giving her free consent: 'I am the Lord's servant... May it be to me according to your word' (Luke 1:38).

Servant leadership is not about giving up our personhood or abdicating responsibility; nor is it about being passive. Jesus may appear to be passive, as the lamb led to the slaughter, the sheep who before his shearers was silent (Isaiah 53:7), but in his ministry he was extremely focused, following what his Father was doing, and making choices about where to go, who to heal, when to go to Jerusalem. He did not wait for others to tell him what to do. It is therefore completely wrong to see servant leadership as 'being a doormat'.

Servant leadership is not, in fact, primarily about serving other people. Women may be used to serving, and some may be used to being at the beck and call of others, but servant leadership is first about service of God and then, through serving God, serving others. Eddie Gibbs helpfully unpacks this distinction:

Sometimes the use of this servant concept has resulted in an abdication of leadership, particularly when it was mistakenly understood to imply that the servant's primary role was to meet the demands of those he or she was called to serve. This is a serious misunderstanding of the servant role of Jesus, who was first and foremost the servant of his heavenly Father.[4]

Philippians 2:5–11

The well-known passage in Philippians 2 perhaps sums up what becoming a servant meant as far as Jesus was concerned. It juxtaposes Jesus' humility with his position and power. Leaders generally hold titles and positions 'over' people, but Jesus 'took the very nature of a servant', and as a servant he epitomizes what leaders should do—lead for the benefit of others.

Leaders seeking to reflect a Christ-like character must exist in a 'paradox of character'. Godly leaders who possess positions of authority must not consider that position 'something to be grasped' (v. 6, NIV), but instead should operate in humility. Authority and humility appear to be mutually exclusive but, with God's help, the two may coexist in the character of a leader, as they did in Christ. This is the heart of Christian leadership.

Then a leader can empty him- or herself. The more a leader possesses a character like Christ, the more they can empty themselves and exhibit extraordinary leadership acts like sacrifice, perseverance, humility and the proper use of power. Christ-like leaders submit their own goals and agenda to the purposes of God, the mission of the organization and the people they lead. Christian leadership is not about how we make our mark but how we write God's story.

There is no doubt that the model of servant is not an easy one, for a whole host of reasons. It may have become distorted by misuse but that does not mean it is not the best model to follow. For Christian leaders, both women and men, it is the only model to follow, but we have much to learn about how to live it. Perhaps it will take the combined wisdom of men and women as leaders to come nearer to what Christ intended servant leadership to be.

THE LEADER AND POWER

Penny Jamieson pointed out in her book *Living at the Edge* (Mowbray, 1997) that one of the difficulties for women leaders is a suspicion of power. The issue of power is thrown into focus when women, the ones over whom power is often held, assume power within areas normally reserved for men. Indeed, some women have at times rejected anything that they have seen as smacking of male religious power, looking instead for the divine feminine, or at an avoidance of leadership and any kind of 'power over'.

Institutional power is often associated with repression and control; it seems to have autonomy and lack accountability. I can well remember the reaction of one vicar, who was challenged about his autocratic attitude. 'I'm not accountable to anyone except God', he said, 'and God has sent me here'—which seemed to mean he could do as he liked. Power gained in leadership is all too often directed toward the benefit of the person in power, not their followers, and is used to gain even more power and authority. Is this the kind of power we expect in Christian leaders?

Until the 20th century, power was mainly a male preserve because men (and it was often white men) had the power to preserve it for themselves. Since then, there have been all kinds of contenders for power. It has often looked as though the only way to gain power is to struggle for it—which in itself involves power—and we can see this happening over and over again, whether in a secular context such as the struggle for women's suffrage or the abolition of apartheid, or in a Christian one, as women have campaigned for the right to be ordained priest. For many campaigners, even being involved in such a struggle for 'power' was a contradiction—but was there any other way? Those without power, whether women or other 'powerless' groups of people, have a dilemma. Do they wait until those with power give it up freely? Given the potentially corrosive nature of power, that may never happen. Or do they struggle to gain a share of that power for themselves?

Fearing power

Many women fear power. They may ask themselves three questions:[5]

- Do I have the ability to do this right?
- Do I have the strength to stand up to others to get the job done?
- Do I have God's permission to exercise power as a Christian woman?

Most women fear the abuse of power in the hands of others. Being physically weaker (in general), women are often more sensitive to the misuse of power and have often been on the receiving end of abuse of power. Many women in leadership in the Church are sitting on stories of personal abuse. So if women become leaders, there is a danger that, as Penny Jamieson put it, 'we become what we hate'.[6] If women are anxious about corrupt power and so shy away from power altogether, in the process they may fail to use God's gifts and fall short of fulfilling God's calling.

Defining power

What is power? There are at least two words used for power in the New Testament. *Dunamis* denotes might, force or strength, and can also mean ability or capability. *Exousia* can mean ability or capability, and also encompasses freedom of choice and the right to decide or to act—as when Jesus freely chose to lay down his life (John 10:18). The philosopher Bertrand Russell defined power as the ability to compel obedience.

What is power about? Is it about winners and losers, or is it about the energy to get things done? Research shows that men are more likely to see power as a discrete quantity. The object of the game is to come out on top—to win, not lose. Many women, on the other hand, are not interested in competitive games. They don't take so easily to power struggles for domination and victory, which may get the adrenaline going but leave women feeling uncomfortable. Even decisions like standing for election to some kind of post, or to a regional or national ministry grouping, may make some women feel uncomfortable: if they are elected, others will lose out. Yet, for many men, competing seems to be the way they establish their identity.

If we bear in mind the two New Testament Greek words for power, we can see that it can be one of two kinds: 'power over' or 'power to'. The first of these is the most common, and is the reason why power so often seems problematic, equated with domination and coercion. Even 'power over' does not have to be inherently dangerous, however, if it is used for the good of others. God has power over his people, but does not hoard it; he pours it out.

'Power to' is a collaborative kind of power, used to empower others. It too can be misused: it can be used to pit one group against another group, creating an imbalance of 'power over'. Too much emphasis on sharing power can sometimes distract leaders from getting the task done as they focus too much on the process rather than the task. If it is used well, though, it is a more transformative kind of power, releasing a life-giving, enabling force, involving not control but influence.

Traditionally our society has esteemed 'power over' more highly. Yet consider these qualities of Jesus:

- He didn't grasp power for himself but voluntarily laid it aside (Philippians 2:5–11).
- He saw power as necessitating service of others (John 13:3–17).
- He had a unique personal power (Mark 1:22). Real power is not about dominance and control but a personal quality of being one with God and with oneself, having integrity.

For Jesus, power was not limited because it was spent for the good of others; rather, it was unleashed. He enhanced the power of power, as it were, by using it to fulfil its goal: the redemption of humankind. We are not less powerful, nor do we limit our power, if we apply power in ways of serving to the benefit of others, as Jesus did. In the Old Testament (Ezekiel 34:2–10) we see a denunciation of leaders who used power to fatten themselves off God's flock rather than shepherding it. Jesus presented an alternative model of the 'good shepherd', the one who lays down his life for his sheep (John 10:11). Hence, the model of leader as shepherd is closely connected to the picture of leader as servant.

Transforming power

Do women use power differently? There is some evidence that women tend to view power as something to be shared, something that expands as others gain it. This sharing of power can be bad if it is an abdication of leadership, leading to a diffusion of power or a denial that we possess it. But secular research on women as leaders does suggest that many women tend to define power differently: that is, as the ability to use their own talents and control their own lives. Christians would see this sharing of power as relational, a model of power that draws energy from the theology of the mutuality of the Trinity. As Leighton Ford puts it, 'True leadership means to receive power from God and to use it under God's rule to serve people in God's way.'[7]

This sharing of power seems to be evident in the work of many women leaders. Frances Hesselbein, who for a number of years was chief executive of the Girl Scouts of the USA, organized the national and regional Girl Scout staff in a way that made use of a circular management structure rather than a hierarchical one. Circles of staff and volunteers were woven together by multiple lines of communication, so power did not move up and down a ladder of authority but in a more diffuse way. Authority came from connection rather than position and power at the 'top'.

One woman minister wrote:

Using power to empower others is my default mode of leadership. I like to work with teams in my church, to give people information and move towards a consensus. I do not have to be at every meeting; others are given the power to make decisions. Power shared is power multiplied; as more and more people in the church share in leadership, they grow in confidence, discover new gifts, and the church is transformed.[8]

Another woman priest had struggled with the word 'power', and wrote:

At first it felt very strange to be speaking about exercising power. The word had such negative associations for me: male, exclusive and hierarchical... but I began to see that power could be an enabling force, something which can be given away. It's a myth that there is only a limited amount to go round. The proper exercise of power creates more power and more creative ways of using it.[9]

Other women have moved to the margins of the Church in order to exercise a ministry less tarnished by the power inherent in what they see as an innately hierarchical institution. One woman became a university chaplain:

I developed a model of ministry based on being on the margin and without power. If we are to be a missionary Church in a postmodern society we will need to let go of our power and learn to live effectively on the margins. That's where the love of God meets the need of the world. [10]

Some material suggests that women can only blame themselves for their lack of power, and should try to find strategies for overcoming their dependency and need to be taken care of by others. Women's failure to achieve real equality, it is argued, is due to their being insufficiently eager for worldly power—and they need to develop more ambitious attitudes. Some feminist writers have suggested that women must deal with their fears about using power, reclaiming their 'dark side' and taking possession of a girlhood will to power. But this is not the way of Jesus. For the Christian, it is all too obvious that women as well as men can succumb to the temptations surrounding power.

While some women are discovering new ways of using power to empower others rather than elevate themselves, women in power can behave just like men in power. Women, like men, have the ability to be good or bad, generous or cruel, and need to confront their ability to dominate and exclude. Women were once regarded as the 'naturally' gentler sex. While that stereotype may be dead and buried, gentleness is still part of the fruit of the Spirit. But it should come as no surprise that we see 'power women' in politics, in business and on screen, and some younger women church leaders want to demonstrate their newfound 'power' in very vocal ways. One priest writes about how she has reflected on the 'shadow side' of priesthood: '... the issues around power, status and control. And I've seen those things, and the temptation to those things in me, and in others—both male and female'. [11]

The powerless leader?

It is, as we have seen, generally assumed that leaders have power, but is that really true? Some fascinating work has been done in this area by Mary Evans, until recently Vice Principal of the London School of

Theology. She used the film *Chicken Run* to contrast the different styles of leadership and power exercised by Rocky, a rooster with an ego bigger than his tail feathers, and Ginger, a hen who seeks out the opinions of others to form a community-based plan and turns out to be the more effective leader: 'Ginger has no power, no authority. But Ginger is a leader who enables people to reach their full potential. Leadership for Christians is never about the matter of claimed authority, status, or power. From the beginning, it was supposed to be a matter of servanthood.'[12]

In the New Testament, words for power and authority are nearly always associated with mutuality, with weakness or with suffering, except when applied to God or secular rulers. Evans challenges us: do we take seriously enough Christ's example of giving up power when it comes to leadership? Do we see leadership as empowering, not controlling? Henri Nouwen writes of 'the most important quality of Christian leadership of the future': 'It is not a leadership of power and control, but a leadership of powerlessness and humility, in which the suffering servant of God, Jesus Christ, is made manifest.'[13]

From the view that power is about the powerful controlling the powerless, to a view that power shared only increases and empowers those who use it and those who are given it, may this vision, this concept of synergy, seen though biblical eyes, point to the way forward.

QUESTIONS FOR REFLECTION AND DISCUSSION

- What does being a servant leader mean for you?
- Why do you think John 13 stands out as one of the most remarkable actions ever recorded?
- How should Christian leaders handle the power inherent in leadership?
- How do you handle people who don't want to lead collaboratively? What strategies could you use to create synergy?

Chapter 7

BUILDING CONFIDENCE AND COURAGE

'The main struggles I've faced while I have been involved in leadership are due to my own insecurities. When I focus on me, and who I am, rather than who God is, I can easily become discouraged and feel quite useless as a leader.'

EMILY, A LEADER IN HER 20s[1]

Ask a 21st-century woman how she feels about herself and answers will vary. Some women will say that they are very happy with who they are. Many, however, don't like themselves—the way they look, or some aspect of their character. Some will even say, 'I hate myself.' Some Christian women think that God loves everyone except them. Whether it's through a long history of being 'second', 'other' or the 'spare rib', many women feel they are less valuable, less worthy than men. In addition, they often feel they have to attain impossible expectations, whether that means being a clothes size 0 (in practice, anorexic), or juggling the duties of paid work with being a daughter, wife and mother. Other women have been abused, rejected or otherwise emotionally damaged.

I have on my desk a book subtitled 'Raising confident and courageous daughters'. With girls now overtaking boys at school, lack of confidence is no longer an issue only for women and girls, but sometimes for men and boys, too. But as I have listened to and read about women leaders, these two issues do seem to be particularly problematic for women: confidence (the focus of much of this chapter) and courage.

CONFIDENCE

The bedrock of success

In the book by Susan Vinnicombe and John Bank, *Women with Attitude: Lessons for Career Management,* the authors explore the careers of six women in the corporate or public sector who have 'made it' to the top. Confidence is top of the list of ten factors for success that emerge from the experiences of these women. And many women who have emerged as leaders testify to the fact that confidence, the key to self-esteem, was vital to their success.

Dame Marjorie Scardino, CEO of Pearson, recalls, 'I was fortunate enough to have parents who did not think that there were any limits to what you could do. No one told me that girls didn't do this, that or the other.'[2] I personally found that one of the advantages of going to an all-girls school was that there were no assumptions about what girls could do. As far as I was aware, all subjects and career paths were open to women. Patricia Vaz, an executive director, writes, 'My mother said women could do anything a man could do and I was determined to prove that she was right.'[3]

Confidence and courage are necessary for every field of leadership. Confidence affects how we perform. It helps us to avoid self-doubt of the kind that can render us unable to move forward. It helps us resist or overcome the barriers we encounter as women in leadership. It affects how others see us, which is a vital aspect of leadership, since leadership implies having others who follow us. People form opinions of us quickly, and confidence, or lack of it, communicates itself. If you are choosing someone for a job and you are thinking, 'Can the person do this job? Will she take the initiative and provide the leadership we need?' you look partly at the person's level of confidence in their own ability and the level of confidence they convey.

Defining confidence

What is confidence? It seems to be a feeling about ourselves, which can change for various reasons and is linked to self-esteem. As we experience success in different aspects of life—our relationships, our career, our service of others and our ministry—our self-esteem is boosted. We become more confident of our abilities and more assured that our efforts will have positive outcomes. In turn, our inner attitude of confidence affects our ability to perform our job, as well as all kinds of things we do in life; we do them better, in turn we feel good about ourselves, and so on.

Leaders become leaders because they have a certain level of competence and confidence. Confidence to take action in front of others, to take responsibility, is essential to leadership. Leaders need the conviction that they have some control over their lives and that they can influence the world about them. People who are confident think positively, then act positively—and are likely to enjoy life and accomplish their aims.

Christian confidence

For a Christian, confidence is rooted in God. It comes from being secure in our identity as members of the covenant relationship with God through Jesus which is at the heart of the Christian faith. It also comes from a sense of call, rooted in the sense that God calls each of his children individually, that he has a purpose for each one, and that he longs for us to use our God-given potential for his purposes. Finally, our confidence flows from our competence as leaders. As we get to know ourselves better, realizing who God has created us to be and the gifts, strengths, and passions he has given us, we will know the kind of environment in which we will lead best. Our competence is strengthened as we reflect on where we need additional knowledge, and as we learn new skills or sharpen existing ones. And part of our responsibility to 'lead diligently'

(Romans 12:8) is to ensure that we continue to learn, grow and develop as leaders.

Confidence is necessary for leadership, including *Christian* leadership. If women are going to lead more like Jesus, they will need confidence and courage. Yet women, and Christian women in particular, often seem to lack confidence. Why is this?

Are women different?

In her review of Fay Weldon's book *What Makes Women Happy*, Helen Brown takes issue with much of the book but agrees 'that women doubt themselves. We do. Possibly more than men. Or at least more openly. And then we phone friends and family who reassure us and buy us drinks and say we are loved'.[4]

It has been shown in a variety of contexts that many men overestimate their abilities and many women underestimate them. This has been demonstrated in children's own assessments of how they are performing at school and at college (despite the likelihood that girls will be performing better than boys), and it clearly affects how women and men feel they are performing in their work. Studies have also shown that women are more likely than men to be dependent on others and to have difficulty in establishing their identity. The fact that some women feel the need to please others can be a barrier to confidence because, unlike men, who often want to compete, they may be more interested in what others think and therefore act in a way that will make them feel accepted.

Sally Helgesen observes, 'I find it often takes a woman ten years longer than men to realize how good they really are. I don't think you can make a contribution until you've moved *beyond* wondering if you're good enough. So I try to give them opportunities to discover that, occasions to build their confidence.'[5] Later in the book, Helgesen argues that in order to use your voice, you must find it. It seems obvious that women take longer to find their voice because most women work in structures that were not devised by them and are weighted in ways that do not reflect their values.

Imposter syndrome

Someone recently told me that she enjoyed both her last and her current jobs, but that every day for the first year or so of each, she had said to herself, 'Today's the day they're going to find out I'm no good at this.' Another woman used almost exactly the same words: appointed to a job as leader of a Christian community, she often felt, 'I can't do this, and one day they'll find me out.'

This is another example of how women find their confidence undermined, and it has been named 'imposter syndrome'. I've heard men admit to feeling like this, but it seems much more common for women and is generally more common than most of us think. The leadership writer Marcus Buckingham defines imposter syndrome as 'the suspicion that we are not as good as everyone says that we are, that our successes may have been accidental, and that, consequently, we may not be entirely sure how to repeat them'.[6]

If we've felt like this, the chances are that, almost by definition, we won't talk about it. We move into a leadership role but feel we don't quite belong there. We're in some sense an interloper, a pretender, and this is likely to reduce our confidence in our ability to do the task God has called us to do.

Pride, humility and confidence

Thanks to the machinations of a male-based psychology, which, as we have seen, still pervades society and to some extent the Church, pride and humility can be gender-specific qualities. Men have traditionally been expected to be proud, women to be humble, and these qualities are commended and reinforced. Our self-image is constructed from a variety of things, including what others tell us and, if we are Christians, what God tells us. But the influence of others is powerful. Oppressed people tend to become what the dominant class defines them to be; they live down to the stunted expectations that society has of them—and women may become what men want them to be.

At one time, women were told that they could not run marathons, so they did not try to run them. They were told that girls were no good at maths and science, so they did not try; they were told (and some are still told) that women could not be leaders—and some believed that too. They may also experience God's call on their lives, but somewhere inside is a mass of contradictions. No wonder women may lack confidence as leaders!

Emily, quoted at the beginning of this chapter, found her confidence undermined by questions about her leadership role:

Occasionally when I have led meetings or taught in church I have had guys come up to me after the service quoting parts of the Bible that appear not to encourage women in leadership. I've had people ask things like, 'Who gives you authority as a girl to stand up in the front and speak?' This has been quite a struggle and a real challenge for me to answer them graciously.[7]

I am aware from conversations with many women in Christian leadership that such challenges to their leadership sap their confidence.

'Not thinking too highly'

Without wishing to make too broad a generalization, I've met more men than women in Christian leadership with too high a view of themselves, and more women with too low a view of themselves. Of course it may be that some men's loud, brash exterior is just a different way of covering up lack of confidence, but I've talked to a number of people in the Church of England about this, and I suspect it applies in other church contexts. Men tend to look at a job advertisement or job description, see that some of it is outside their current experience and think, 'Oh, I'm sure I could do that.' Women are more likely to look at the same information, realize that there are a few things beyond their experience and think, 'I couldn't possibly do that.' Even if someone phones them up and says, 'Would you like to apply for this post?' they may still say, 'No, I really don't think I could do it.'

In Romans 12:3, Paul writes, 'Do not think of yourself more highly than you ought', and some leaders need to hear that. Other Christians have deep-rooted feelings of inferiority—and John Stott suggests that Paul might have added that we must avoid too low an estimate of ourselves as well as too high an estimate.[8] The verse goes on to call the Roman believers to think about themselves 'with sober judgment, according to the faith God has distributed to each of you', and then speaks about gifts. In other words, God has given us gifts and he wants us to recognize and use them.

In either case, what Paul wants Christians to do is to learn to rely on God and have a right view of ourselves, seeing ourselves as God sees us—as gifted children, but weak and incomplete without his Spirit and his power.

There are two final points to bear in mind. Some of those who teach in theological colleges and courses, preparing women and men for authorized ministry, have observed the lack of confidence in some women as a concern. An interesting theory is that the Church attracts those lacking in confidence in the first place—and it is from these people that God calls out leaders. Ever since the days of the early Church, part of the attraction of the Christian faith is that God calls nobodies and makes them somebodies, but such people may still be, humanly speaking, lacking in confidence.

Then there is the subjective nature of confidence. It is more common for people to say that they lack confidence than to feel they have too much of it. Confidence seems to be a commodity in short supply, and it's something that many leaders are looking for. When my colleagues in CPAS and I read applications and references for the Arrow Leadership Programme, many of the women (and some of the men, too) mention 'hoping to gain in confidence' as one of their goals for the programme. These are outwardly competent leaders, who perceive that growing in confidence is vital to their development as a leader.

Why is self-doubt so damaging?

Lack of confidence is damaging in a number of ways:

- We try to prove ourselves worthy by filling our lives fuller and fuller with things we know we can do: I'm good at visiting—I'll do lots of that; I'll work hard—I must be achieving something. This can distort our ministry and stop us moving on.
- The converse is that we don't do the things we should be doing: we procrastinate and avoid situations that make us anxious.
- We look to others to gain our sense of purpose and identity, and become people-pleasers. We find it hard to say 'no' because we want people to like us—that's where we get our esteem from. Again, this distorts our ministry.
- Alternatively, we fill our lives with escapist activities or addictions or material things to hide the pain.

Management scholar Rosabeth Moss Kanter has defined confidence as 'the sweet spot between arrogance and despair'.[9] This sums up the delicate tension in confidence, which is perhaps why it is problematic for many women. What is appropriate confidence? How do we come to a place where we have appropriate confidence— neither a paralysing lack of self-belief and self-worth, which results in despair, nor the conviction that we can do anything and nothing will stand in our way, which leads to arrogance?

Biblical self-esteem

Look along the shelves of self-help books in any bookshop or on internet book sale sites and you can see them—shedloads of books on how to build confidence: *The Confidence Coach*, *Creating Self-Esteem*, *Building Confidence for Dummies*. Their recipe for confidence tends to be based either on looking outside ourselves towards achievement and success in life or on looking inwards. 'Believe in yourself; know your worth,' we are told. 'Be a winner'; 'take charge'; get beyond your self-limiting beliefs and you can do anything you want. Biblical confidence, on the other hand, is based on looking not outwards to achievements or into ourselves, but upwards—towards God and the risen Christ.

Jesus' confidence came from knowing who he was: 'And a voice came from heaven, "You are my Son, whom I love; with you I am well pleased"' (Mark 1:11). That was his security, and he was confident in his Father's love for him and affirmation of him. Our confidence comes from knowing that we are loved, we are called and, through Jesus, God is pleased with us.

Paul wrote to the Christians in Corinth, 'Such confidence we have through Christ before God. Not that we are competent in ourselves to claim anything for ourselves, but our competence comes from God. He has made us competent as ministers' (2 Corinthians 3:4–6). This reminds us that without God we are nothing, but with him we are everything. God has given us many natural talents and he has gifted us in unique ways. Acknowledging our natural talents and spiritual gifts, and learning to rejoice in them, use them and develop them, helps to give us a right confidence.

We therefore depend on God in a number of ways:

- as the giver of all things.
- as the sustainer of our ministry.
- as the one who does spiritual work in people's lives.

Depending on God, we acknowledge that we are clay jars and therefore weak, and that without his help we can easily lose heart and give up.

When I was ordained priest and had a special service where I presided for the first time at Communion, the friend whom I asked to preach chose a passage from 2 Corinthians 4, and called his sermon 'Christians, carrier bags and not losing heart'. Carrier bags, he argued, are today's equivalent of Paul's 'jars of clay'—items that are easily broken, disposable. But we carry treasure that is beyond price.

This dependence on God should lead us to a right sense of competence, one that comes from God: 'He has made us competent as ministers' (2 Corinthians 3:6).

Content in all circumstances

Paul's letter to the Philippians can be read as an extended commentary on Christian self-esteem.[10] Paul was imprisoned for the sake of Christ but he remained remarkably confident. This attitude was based not on his situation, however, but on what God could do with it (1:13). He wrote, 'I will continue to rejoice' (v. 18); we can have confidence that whatever happens, God will be able to use us.

False modesty, insisting that we are of no value to God, is not humility; it is an insult to the Father who made us. Paul wrote, 'In humility value others above yourselves' (2:3), but this does not mean that humility is about devaluing ourselves; it means having a positive evaluation of others. Paul looks to Christ and his death on the cross: Christ became as we are, so that we can be as he is. He came down to share our human life, so that we can share his divine life. We can rejoice with the psalmist that 'You have made [human beings] a little lower than the heavenly beings and crowned them with glory and honour. You made them rulers over the works of your hands; you put everything under their feet' (Psalm 8:5–6).

Towards the end of Philippians, Paul writes these much-quoted words: 'I can do all this through him who gives me strength' (4:13). Paul is convinced that he can do all that God calls him to do, 'in him'—that is, in the power of God, using the gifts and talents he has been given. Paul wrote the most joy-filled, upbeat letter in the New Testament while in circumstances that most of us would have found impossible. How does he manage this? His confidence is in God, not in himself, so he is not dismayed by circumstances but sees the bigger picture—the victory of God over every circumstance, even death.

We may think, 'I do trust in God. I know I have some competence —leadership is one of my spiritual gifts, and people tell me I'm a good leader—but I don't *feel* at all confident.' That is because competence is fairly objective: we can measure talent, gifts and skills; we can know what we know, and learn more; we can gain experience. But confidence is about feelings. No matter how many sermons we hear about finding our confidence in God, no matter how much competence we have, we may not feel confident. If that is how we feel, what can we do to grow into a right confidence in God and a just estimate of ourselves?

How to gain in confidence

- We can gain in competence, becoming more aware of our strengths, how to build on them, and how to manage our weaknesses. We can add to our skills and knowledge. When we have done something a number of times, we can then be more confident about doing it next time.
- We may need to practise or rehearse, prepare thoroughly for what we are going to do. It is all too easy to look at others who seem to 'perform' confidently and forget that they may have been a leader for many years and have put in hours of practice themselves.
- We can use a mentor or coach to discuss areas of competence or particular difficulties in our ministry context.

- We can strengthen our sense of calling, being reminded of our uniqueness in Christ and right dependence on him. To do this, we might want to meditate on particular scriptures or take a quiet day and ask God to show us if there are any barriers from which he wants to release us.
- For some leaders, lack of confidence is largely the result of emotional damage in childhood or past negative experiences, which have affected our sense of competence or call, or both. We may need to seek healing or counselling to deal with this damage, or we may have to accept that some weakness in this area is like Paul's 'thorn in the flesh' (2 Corinthians 12:7), throwing us into increased dependence on God.

The confidence required to lead comes from learning about ourselves—our skills, prejudices, talents, shortcomings and leadership style. Confidence develops as we build on strengths and overcome weaknesses, which comes from having goals, taking risks, holding to convictions and building an arsenal of small successes and failures. Our successes convince us that it is possible to succeed. Our failures teach us that it is possible to fail, yet go on.

Eleanor Roosevelt once said, 'Nobody can make you feel inferior without your consent.' She was right. Having the confidence to experience life's failures and successes is critical to those in leadership positions, but ultimately we grow in confidence through valuing ourselves in and through Christ.

Rather than meditating on self-help affirmations like 'I am good enough' or 'I can do it', we can meditate instead on scriptures from Hosea 11:1, 3–4 and Isaiah 43:1–5a, inserting our own name to make them God's personal word to us. Other suitable verses for meditation are Joshua 1:9, Psalm 27:1 and Psalm 56:3–4.

COURAGE

What is courage?

Courage is also a key to effective leadership. A dictionary definition of courage is 'the ability to disregard one's fear, bravery'. This makes it closely allied to confidence, which in some senses is the opposite of fear. Our call (knowing who we are and what God has called us to do) and character (growing in Christ-like character) should result in courage.

John Adair includes courage as one of the chief qualities associated with leaders, and a quality that can be discerned in Jesus, who, for much of his ministry, was a marked man and finally had to face the cross.[11] Two lists of leadership qualities include 'courage', not just because it is one of a number of words beginning conveniently with 'C' but because courage really is an essential aspect of leadership. According to one of these lists, courage involves being 'willing to stand up for one's own beliefs, challenge others, admit mistakes, change one's behaviour when necessary'.[12] Another list of ten keys to effective leadership includes 'Courage—overcoming the fear of failure.'[13]

Stephen Covey, best known for his book *The Seven Habits of Highly Effective People,* in another book, *First Things First*, links confidence and courage together in an 'upward spiral'. Setting and working towards principle-based goals is an act of courage. When we set out to do so confidently, in hopeful expectation of positive results, we experience growth.

Are women courageous?

Courage is not a quality with which all women immediately identify. Sandra Walston, an American who has studied women in relation to the concept of courage, found that in a survey of 700 women only a handful chose 'courageous' from a list of adjectives they were offered to describe themselves. In her research she has found that society rarely recognizes women as courageous and women rarely see themselves as possessing courage. Perhaps this is because many have been socialized to believe that courage, like power, is not meant to be part of the feminine nature.[14]

For men, courage often seems to be related to keeping their autonomy and being strong and in charge, facing down danger. Yet the root of the word 'courage' is the Old French *corage*, which means 'heart and spirit'. If courage is defined as any act that requires inner strength, women may be more able to identify circumstances in their lives that have required courage. Walston's research and personal experience revealed that women who did own courage were much better equipped to deal with everyday life than those who did not. Women often have to face huge emotional, physical and psychological crises: abuse, betrayal, violence, unwanted pregnancy, discrimination. If they rename the inner strength they have found to overcome these crises as courage, they may come to see that they *do* have this essential leadership quality.

Leaders need courage because leadership is about change. It takes courage to be first off, not sure if those you lead will follow, or to lead in a direction where you're sure not everyone wants to go. Leadership may well entail taking people not only to a place they have never been to before, but somewhere we've never been to either. As Walston puts it, 'Leadership requires the courage to walk in the dark.'[15]

Courage to stand out

The courage a leader needs may be a mixture of emotional courage and moral courage. Moral courage means being willing to take hard decisions, to do the right thing even when you know it will be unpopular. That's the kind of courage Daniel showed when he vowed not to eat and drink the Babylonian royal food, which had probably been offered to idols (Daniel 1:8), and when he kept on praying to God despite the king's edict (6:10).

I remember that when the city council for which my dad worked declared itself a 'nuclear-free zone', he stood up and spoke his mind (which he was not supposed to do), rather than just accepting the stance of the decision makers. The rights and wrongs of that particular argument are not the point. His point was, while being nuclear-free might be an ideal, did not loving your neighbour mean putting in place realistic steps to defend people from aggression? As someone who had fought in a world war, he was not impressed by what he saw as naïve posturing. That took courage.

I guess I have followed in his footsteps, though I've not thought about it much. In one church I earned respect for having principles rather than wanting to be popular (it was a church where some of my theological convictions were quite at odds with those of the congregation). I've not been afraid to challenge 'powers that be' in the wider church, whether about the priority of mission or scripture, or the importance of inclusive language.

Jochabed, the mother of Moses, showed courage when she hid her infant son in defiance of the king's order to kill all Hebrew baby boys. The midwives Shiphrah and Puah (two of my favourite biblical characters) showed similar courage when they defied the king to his face, because they 'feared God' more than they feared the king of Egypt (Exodus 1:17). Courage is about putting God's will above our human fears, and trusting that he will be with us.

Safer than a known way

Courage is not the absence of fear: courage assumes fear. It may well involve something like the catchphrase (which comes from the book of that title by Susan Jeffers) 'Feel the fear and do it anyway'—except that, when we talk about courage in Christian leadership, it's not about random risk-taking, stepping out into the dark. It's more like stepping out and knowing that our hand is in the hand of God, as described in the famous meditation by Minnie Louise Haskins, quoted by King George VI in his Christmas broadcast in 1939:

'Go out into the darkness
and put your hand into the hand of God.
That shall be to you
Better than light
And safer than a known way.'

Many of the stories told in the magazine of the Barnabas Fund (which supports Christians who are persecuted for their faith) are of what I would call real courage. A 21-year-old woman from North Korea converted to Christianity and returned to her country. She was arrested for sharing the gospel and continued to evangelize her jailers while in prison. She explained that she prayed for her country because she loved it and its people—and, remarkably, she was released. Another news item told how the widow of a murdered Christian worker forgave the killers, reading Luke 23:34: 'Father, forgive them, for they do not know what they are doing.'[16] That is courage.

What stops us being courageous? Fear of failure? At the risk of using stereotypes, I wonder if that's more of a problem for men than for women. Women are less often out to prove something, to compete, or (dare I say it) to 'show off'. Women are less likely to risk the 'big event', the slightly risky enterprise, when there may be other ways of achieving the same result. But women who have given birth probably know more about courage than those who associate it only with bungee jumping and fast motorbikes.

Leaders not only need to be courageous, they need to be able to instil courage into those who follow them. Sometimes leaders have done this by leading from the front—'going into battle', as it were, like a general leading an army—but that is not the only way to engender courage. Sometimes leaders can instil courage just as effectively by admitting their fears and weakness in human terms and encouraging their people to seek God's will and walk in it.

Many leaders lack the courage to say 'no', yet this is just as crucial to good leadership as the courage to say 'yes'. Leaders need to be able to say 'no' when others ask of them things that they know are not God's will for them. Jesus (implicitly) said 'no' to some people every time he said 'yes' to others. It takes courage to say 'no' to things that may make us popular with people, especially when God's 'yes' will make us unpopular.

It may also take courage to face current reality. In Britain we are constantly reminded that we face an uncertain future unless we change and 'do church' differently. In an Anglican context (and it's the same for most of the denominations), unless we change, we will die. We face the choice between a comfortable death—if that is not a contradiction in terms—and an uncomfortable life. Many church leaders find it easier to ignore reality and give their followers what they want. They may argue, 'People might stop giving if I start to confront them with reality', or, 'People will leave the church.' Do we have the courage as leaders to make uncomfortable choices for the sake of his kingdom? Do we have the courage to close churches, reorganize church life, wind up committees or organizations, do whatever needs to be done, for the sake of people who do not know God?

Every leader needs the courage to dream. What are our dreams? And do we have the courage to reach for them, work for them, pray for them and see God bring them to being?[17]

It takes courage to face the forces of darkness in the spiritual battle. It takes courage to face the truth about yourself as a leader, your talents and strengths, and the gaps and weaknesses you have to manage or work around. It takes courage to keep going when those around you bail out or give up, lose their first love, go off the boil or sell out for an easier way. Jesus went to the cross—for us—with courage. One of my friends sometimes reminds me, 'The Lamb wins!' Whatever life throws at us, that should give us confidence to trust him and courage to live the leadership roles he gives us.

QUESTIONS FOR REFLECTION AND DISCUSSION

- Can you acknowledge your talents, gifts and accomplishments?
- What can you do to strengthen your confidence in who God has made you and where he has called you to serve?
- Do you think of yourself as a courageous person? Why, or why not? If not, what would help you to 'own' the courage you surely do have?
- As a leader, what is your greatest fear? How can you deal with it so that you lead with confidence and courage?

Chapter 8

STEPPING UP TO LEAD

'The female advantage is having plenty of choices. The female burden is having to make them.'[1]

'You cannot be anything you want to be—but you can be a lot more of who you are already.'[2]

God calls women to step up to leadership but they often lag behind men in developing as leaders, and some factors, relating particularly to them as women, continue to present challenges. Gretchen Englund, who mentors women leaders, writes this:

Even the most confident-appearing woman can struggle with a sense of low self-esteem. Stemming from one's skewed view of God's acceptance and delight in her, she questions her own worth and doubts who she is. She is a called woman leader who is clearly called of God, but who inwardly struggles with questions of self-doubt, personal shame, and quietly wonders whether God's delight in her is really true…

Women leaders—again because of the many layers of a woman's life—need to address their inner anxiety before they can freely move to the next level… Women can have an internal tornado, full of questions and unfinished business: Am I okay? Am I really competent? What about being single? Are my kids doing well? Does my husband find delight in me? Am I doing life right?[3]

How do women become equipped to be the leaders God wants them to be? This book has already explored a number of issues, including the mixed messages they receive because of unresolved theological

172

issues: is it biblical for them to lead? Chapter 6 explored some of the issues around power and service, and Chapter 7 considered the need for women to gain confidence and courage. This chapter explores some of the barriers to women's development as leaders, suggests some ways in which those barriers can be removed, and focuses on two additional key areas—being intentional about development by compiling a 'life vision', and finding support through the transitions of leadership by the use of mentoring.

As with the rest of this book, it's a chapter for women *and* men. There are some practical suggestions for women, most of which could also apply to men, and I hope that male leaders will learn more about how to help their Christian sisters to use their leadership gifts for the kingdom.

MESSAGES WE SEND OUR DAUGHTERS

The messages women imbibe, which may lead them to doubt their calling as leaders, start young. Early adolescence is the time when many girls begin to 'silence' themselves, letting others speak for them and allowing other voices to usurp the value of their own voice. Thus there is a need to start young if we are to develop girls into confident leaders.

Christian literature for teenage girls sometimes encourages them to take submissive roles in their relationship with young men. For example, one special edition of the New Testament for teenage girls says, 'Guys need to step up and be the man; you need to be the woman.'[4] The message sent to girls is that men are only men if women remain passive. One writer encourages women to 'embrace mature femininity' by encouraging and making room for men to practise servant leadership: 'If a man's biggest temptation is to be passive, a woman's biggest temptation is to take control.'[5] Women are encouraged to let men initiate and lead, even in ordinary conversation.

For some young women, even the symbolism of worship can reinforce their sense of being in a secondary position. I recently worshipped in an Anglican church where the service began with eight men processing in—two priests and a variety of assistants, such as the crucifer (carrying the cross) and acolytes (carriers of candles). For that church it was normal, but among the worshippers were a number of teenage girls from a nearby girls' boarding school. What message were they receiving?

Different forces compete for the attention of children from a young age, hence the need to give Christian children good foundations in their faith. As the 'pinkness' into which girls are now indoctrinated influences more and more areas of their lives, one publisher is fighting back. It's great that Pupfish, a publisher of colourful books for young children, should bring out four books on biblical women to go alongside those on four men in a series of *First Word Heroes*.

At first sight, the books on Martha, Ruth, Miriam and Esther look pink and glittery—because the covers *are* pink and glittery! But inside, the stories are told simply (for toddlers), with the message that Miriam didn't allow the elevation and dazzle of a princess to faze her but recognized God's provision and bravely seized the moment. Esther was beautiful—but she was brave as well. Leadership development needs to start at this very young age, because the voices that pull in the opposite direction start equally early.

If God's plan is for women to share with men in the leadership of his Church, then it is important that children and young women receive the message that God calls women as well as men to this role. This argument is not yet won, and in some denominations, churches and groupings, as we have seen, attitudes towards women leaders have hardened rather than becoming more open. At the same time, girls are growing up in a culture where there are very few gender barriers to affect the choices they will make. So life for Christian women may become easier for some but for others it may become more confusing. One young leader wrote:

I went to an all-girls school where we were told we could be and do anything we wanted, that nothing should stand in our way. So it came as quite a shock to me when, as a new Christian at 15, I met a guy who told me that women weren't allowed to teach in church. It didn't make any sense to me, but there was no arguing with this guy—he was convinced!

I went home frustrated and confused. Everything I'd learned and experienced of God so far was about love and freedom, so it seemed strange that he would limit women in the gifts he gave them and the areas of ministry they could engage in. But I wanted to be faithful and obedient to God, and if he really wasn't into women in leadership then I needed to come to terms with that.[6]

There are resources available that would have helped that 15-year-old; they need to reach the hands of those who would value them.

HOW TALENT DEVELOPS

An understanding of how talents and strengths develop can alert us to the need to give children and young people opportunities to exercise leadership. Learning is determined by the network of connections between brain cells, called neurons. In the process of learning, connections between neurons are formed through synapses, and, during a person's life, their neurons will form tens of thousands of synaptic connections with other neurons. What causes these synaptic connections are our genes. To some extent, 'what you can learn and what you can't is determined by what genes you have',[7] and there appears to be some connection between genes and personality. Unlike abilities, knowledge and skills, personality is relatively fixed.

What is important in relation to young people is that the rate of learning slows down in the course of our lives. We are made so that we can absorb maximum learning at a young age—hence it's easier to learn a language at primary school age than when we are older.

Childhood is the optimum time for making new connections in our brains and doing new learning, and adolescence and the early 20s are the latest time when talents are formed. Beyond this, it is very difficult to learn in areas unconnected to the core strengths which have emerged by that stage.

If we want to grow leaders, we need to give children and young people experience of leadership from a young age, otherwise they are much less likely to develop that ability.

Educators are increasingly realizing that the best way of developing leaders is through a combination of leadership experience and reflection on it. There are probably more opportunities now than ever for young people to learn to lead. The family is the place to start, and parents can be proactive in encouraging youngsters to take a lead from an early age. Other opportunities come at school. While schools have more recently come to serve the values of competitive individualism, they still provide opportunities to learn leadership: on school councils, in captaining sports teams, and as class leaders, prefects and head pupils. Organizations such as Girls' Brigade also offer good leadership opportunities for girls.

In churches, some young people enjoy helping to lead younger groups and holiday clubs, while others can lead their peers in cell groups and Christian basics courses, and also learn to lead worship. Several organizations, such as Crusaders, run training in leadership for young people—in some cases, specifically for girls CPAS is working on a course to develop teenagers (14–18s) as leaders.

HOW TO DEVELOP GIRLS AS LEADERS

What a teenage girl learns about her place in church is very important. Girls' self-esteem is generally lower than boys' self-esteem at all ages, and girls' self-esteem plummets from the age of around 10, through adolescence. Thus a key area of focus for developing girls as leaders will be to boost their self-esteem and confidence. Girls as well as women need to be reminded that God made them and, as someone said, 'He don't make junk.' Even when their own view of themselves is low, and they compare themselves unfavourably with others, Christian girls can be transformed through absorbing the truth that God values them, has gifted them and can use them to make a difference to the world around them.

Some research into how to create an atmosphere in which women's leadership in the Church will be more fully accepted advocates a conscious process of education for girls, using techniques that are not competitive but use a more relational style of learning. The key components of such a programme, it is suggested, should be modelling and mentoring.[8]

Modelling

Churches need to model women's leadership in two specific ways: through the language they use and through their placement of women in key leadership positions.

- Be aware of the use of language, in the pulpit and in small groups. Inclusive-language Bibles should be used. Girls need to hear examples of female leaders as well as male leaders, in scripture and in church tradition.
- Key leadership positions: girls need to see leadership as a viable choice for them in their own futures in the Church. If they see women as leaders, they will believe that it is something they can do. If they see only male leaders, they may question whether they can lead, even if they experience God calling them.

Mentoring

Much has been written recently on mentoring young people, and much of the material on mentoring women can also be applied to girls and younger women. External support from non-parental role models is very helpful for girls as they negotiate the complexities of adolescence. Interestingly, some research has found that individual–team mentoring and friend-to-friend mentoring works better with girls than the traditional style of older/younger one-to-one mentoring. It's important to allow girls to learn in groups with other girls, as well as in mixed groups, since on their own they will have the freedom to raise issues at a deeper level. Girls also respond well to one woman leading a group of girls—for example, for a weekly girls' group or girls' night out.

Other areas to address with girls are the 'beauty myths' of our culture, which can encourage them to focus too much attention on being attractive to men. True beauty is more than skin deep and Christian girls need to learn that they are beautiful because they are loved by God, not because they attract the most boys.

Just as Christians are always no more than one generation away from extinction, so are Christian leaders. Those of us who are already leaders are responsible for nurturing, training and equipping those who are following on behind—and making sure that we do not stick around in our leadership positions too long. We need to make space for young leaders to take their turn.

One feature of Generation X (those born between 1965 and 1983) is that they tend to have an inclusive outlook and assume gender equality. Now *their* children are growing up; those young people will assume equality, too. But will they find themselves confronted by different values in the Church—values which I would argue are not biblical but part of a Christian subculture? If we are to see a more truly egalitarian Church, and leadership expressed as a partnership of men and women together, then we need to ensure that girls as well as boys, young women as well as young men, who have gifts and talents for leadership, are given the opportunities to become the leaders God calls them to be.

AMBITION

As girls move into womanhood, they begin to make choices about their lives. One reason why some women are less proactive than men in developing themselves as leaders is the ambivalence associated with the concept of ambition. 'Ambition' has often been problematic for Christians, and especially for women. The word is often used pejoratively, implying egotism, selfishness or the manipulative use of others for one's own ends. Thus women don't admit to being ambitious and may avoid pursuing their dreams, while many men consider ambition to be a necessary and desirable part of their lives.[9]

Women who have appeared to be ambitious have often been judged more harshly than men. One woman writes about the time when, after being in parish worker and then deaconess roles for about twelve years, she longed to be ordained:

I struggled with a Christian attitude to ambition. Some said that women who were seeking ordination were only looking for status. Strangely, that was never said of men. These voices made me examine my own motives. After much thought, discussion, Bible study and prayer, I came to the conclusion that ambition is only wrong if it is selfish and at the expense of others. I genuinely wanted to offer my gifts and experience to the church in a way that would be challenging and stimulating to others as well as myself.[10]

Ambition in itself, then, is not wrong. Paul writes in Romans 15: 20–21, 'Thus I make it my ambition to proclaim the good news, not where Christ has already been named, so that I do not build on someone else's foundation, but as it is written, "Those who have never been told of him shall see, and those who have never heard of him shall understand"' (NRSV). Godly ambition is appropriate.

While some women and men are ambitious today to make a million, have the perfect home or write a bestselling novel, none of these ambitions is as big as what God calls us to—participating in building his kingdom. We need to re-evaluate 'ambition'. If our ambition is rooted in God, then following it is more than appropriate; it is essential.

'WOMEN WHO LOVE TOO MUCH'

It is not just anxiety about ambition that can hinder women who seek to step up to leadership. As we have already seen in Chapter 6, women sometimes see their task as serving others rather than developing themselves. Mary Stewart Van Leeuwen notes that 'one of the main problems of today's psychologists is accounting for women's constant tendency to avoid developing personal self-sufficiency for the sake of preserving even pathological relationships with the opposite sex'.[11] External barriers to women's achievement may be increasingly overcome but there still seem to be internal ones.

Van Leeuwen argues that these tendencies have their origin in the Fall. In Genesis 3, for men dominion became domination, while for women sociability became social enmeshment. Women live out Genesis 3:16—'your desire will be for your husband'—to this day, and many women use the preservation of relationships as an excuse not to exercise accountable dominion. Hence, she suggests, the popularity of self-help books for women with titles such as *Women Who Love Too Much*, *Woman as Victim*, and *Men who Hate Women and the Women who Love Them*.

Some dynamic is at work in women which cannot be eradicated by self-help advice, life coaching, psychotherapy, feminism or institutional change. Nothing less than a radical solution can change it—but that radical solution came in Christ, and we have to work out what that means. On the cross, Satan was defeated and the effects of the Fall, including the domination of men and social enmeshment of women, were reversed. Women will become truly free as they come to know Christ and claim for themselves all that he won for them.

At Pentecost the Holy Spirit was poured out on women as well as men, inaugurating a new era in which women are gifted by God to take their place alongside men. Christian women today live in the light of the 'emancipation proclamation' of Pentecost, but our full healing awaits the inauguration of the new heaven and new earth, when God's kingdom will be fully established.

Another insight comes from those who have explored the biblical concept of 'sin' and its effect on women. Sin has commonly been defined as the unjustified concern of the self for its own power and prestige, and is equated with selfishness. As a result, many women have seen submission to God's will as good and self-assertion as bad. But in an influential essay published in 1960, 'The human situation: a feminine view', the feminist theologian Valerie Saiving argued that such things as triviality, lack of an organizing centre, dependence on others, inability to make decisions for oneself—any negation or underdevelopment of self—may be viewed as sin. In this 'sin of hiding', women run from freedom and pour their energy into the lives of others, failing to live as their own person under God. While I would not want to argue that 'sin' is exclusively gendered in this way, there is some truth in this insight.

Some women may need to repent of their overdependence on others and step up to dependence on God alone, being open to what he calls them to do. Van Leeuwen quotes a fascinating example of this from the time of the abolition movement in America. One abolitionist leader observed how women came to realize that they were holding back the fight against slavery by invoking the excuse of feminine modesty. He wrote to two fellow abolitionists:

The very week I was converted, and the first time I ever spoke in a religious meeting, I urged females both to pray and to speak if they felt deeply enough to do it, and not to be restrained from it by the fact that they were females… The result was that seven female Christians confessed their sin in being restrained by their sex, and prayed publicly in succession that very evening.[12]

Some women may need to repent of unhealthy people-pleasing and deference to the needs of others, and focus, perhaps for the first time, on what God calls them to achieve for him. Two tools which, under God, may be used to do this are outlined at the end of this chapter: a right way to express ambitions or aspirations, and how to focus on making the most of who God has made us to be.

WOMEN AND LIFE STAGES

Another issue that sometimes impedes women as they step up to leadership is that theories of leadership development and career development are mainly based on the experience of men. Some research suggests that women's career paths are different from men's. This is for several reasons:

- The impact of family responsibilities.
- The relational element in women's careers (shown by findings from developmental psychology).
- Constraints on women's careers, causing them to develop in different directions.

While men may fast-track in their 20s and 30s—in business or in a profession—or maybe five to ten years later in the Church, and able leaders will be leading a large church or even becoming a bishop in their 40s, the path for women is different. Research published in 2005 suggested that women's careers are often more pragmatic than men's. Women's lives often progress not in linear ways but in ways that are more organic and guided by opportunity and intuition. Career is not a 'path up' but a series of zigzags.[13]

Life as improvisation

For many women, life could be described as an improvisation. As one woman put it:

Each of us constructs a life that is her own central metaphor for thinking about the world. But of course these lives do not look like parables or allegories. Mostly, they look like ongoing improvisations, quite ordinary sequences of day-to-day events. They continue to unfold... The compositions we create in these times of change are filled with interlocking messages or our commitments and decisions. Each one is a message of possibility.[14]

Women, more than men, have to balance competing claims in their lives; for most women, their overriding concerns are for their career and for others (family and friends). Most women strive to achieve in their lives a balance between work and non-work aspects of life, which takes account of a variety of factors. And for many women there is a constant tension between 'career' and 'relationships with others'; the emphasis between these may change at different points in a woman's life. This picture is very different from the typical image of a career as a lifelong, uninterrupted experience of work, which can be divided up into neat stages of development, starting with ideas about working and ending with retirement—though for many men this pattern is changing too.

Phase 1: Idealistic achievement

In the first phase of their working life, aged 24–35 (I have used the ages given in the 2005 research by O'Neil and Bilimora cited above, but they can be read flexibly), most women have high hopes. They are proactive, they may expect to have a family later, and they view their career as an opportunity to make a difference. Women who embark on Christian ministry in this stage are able to 'go for it' with youthful enthusiasm and total commitment.

Phase 2: Pragmatic endurance

Women may well find themselves, in the next phase (aged 36–45), juggling multiple demands, torn between career and life choices. If they are married, they may have taken a career break to raise children. If they are single, they may be trying to keep their options for the future open, while their zeal for their career has waned and they have to deal with less supportive working environments. This second phase is where women leaders in the Church may struggle most and, if struggling with competing demands is too much, they may drop out. In order that women get a wide range of experience as leaders and the same opportunities as men, it is vital that they have good support.

Phase 3: Reinventive contribution

Finally, in the third phase (46–50 plus), women become relatively free of childcare responsibilities (or have come to terms with the lack of children) and often find a renewed sense of purpose, which makes this a very productive time. They may embark on a new career (for a number of women, this is the time when they are freer to hear God's call to authorized ministry). While some men may be past their peak and looking forward to retirement, women may be reaching their most productive phase—but they all too often find that what few resources there are for leadership development are designed for women and men who started on this path earlier in their lives.

Anita Roddick wrote a few years ago, 'My mother always told me that a woman reinvents herself in her 50s. That's one advantage to being a woman.'[15] At a ministers' meeting, I met one woman, who must have been well over the age of 60, who said with a twinkle in her eye, 'I'm going to be ordained in June—such an exciting opportunity for me!'

Implications for leadership

What does all this mean for women leaders in the Church today? Women in the first phase need to be equipped for ministry for the long haul, so that they are not derailed when they hit the demands of phase 2. In that phase, flexible jobs and working hours may be needed to allow women to retain their working life while raising children. Women will also need challenges to stretch them and support them, and mentoring to help them integrate their lives and build their confidence.

In this phase, women who take a career break from church leadership to bring up children, and who are not in a paid position, may find themselves almost non-ministers so far as the structures are concerned. The skills women bring to the third phase may prove to equip them well for senior leadership posts: their combination of formal and informal experience may give them the skills they need to take on additional responsibility. They will also be valuable as mentors and proactive champions of the women coming along behind them.

Of course, as the patterns of women's lives change, and women have to cope with less opposition and impossible juggling in the second phase, this difference may be lessened.

WORK–LIFE BALANCE

Work–life balance has emerged as a major issue in impeding the career progression of female managers, and in church circles also it poses challenges for women stepping up to leadership. Among those who work very long hours, expectations in the business world may be far greater than those for most paid ministers, but church leaders are traditionally 'on call' all the time, except on days off—and some ministers don't take those.

Some of the tensions for women church leaders are the same as for their counterparts in secular employment—the demands of balancing home and work. I remember well the first words spoken to me when I arrived at my placement church at 7.30 on a Sunday morning. Lorraine was rushing round the kitchen, putting egg on some rolls and the rolls on a plate. 'What I really need is a wife,' she said. She was off to lead three services—at 8.00, 9.30 and 10.30—then had to turn up with her plate for a bring-and-share lunch. Being 'vicar' and 'woman' was a stretch.

Work–life balance is one of the issues identified in research on women as leaders in business and the professions, and, as I have already suggested, policies such as flexible working, child care and family-friendly work policies are making it easier for women. For women leaders in the Church, working from home may make life easier. Women with children at school may be able to fit the 'school run' in with other duties; it is becoming more acceptable for women (and men) to time meetings around this responsibility. On the other hand, low stipends or salaries make paid child care impossible for many women. The debate continues about how many plates women can spin without collapsing, and the answer will be different in each case. Women leaders in the Church, as in any other context, need to learn good time management, how to recognize and deal with stress, and how to live in 'seasons'—times when life is very busy, alternated with times that are less pressured.

THE STAINED-GLASS CEILING

Over the last 20 or 30 years, women have moved into the professions and every area of business and commercial life. Yet there is still a lack of women in senior posts, whether we are looking at directors of the FTSE 100 companies or head teachers. This has been termed the 'glass ceiling'.

In business and the professions, women have not moved into senior leadership in a way that we might have predicted. In 2006,

30 years after the Sex Discrimination Act 1976, women still made up only 9 per cent of the judiciary, 10 per cent of senior police officers and 13 per cent of national newspaper editors. While initially we might have expected the weight of numbers in the professions to filter down (or up), it is clear that other forces have been at work.

In many churches, it is the same situation—a stained-glass ceiling, as it were. Women and men both serve as leaders of churches, yet when it comes to senior leadership roles in most denominations, the majority of posts are held by men. There are, as we have seen, theological reasons for this, but even where churches or denominations are theoretically in support of women's leadership, the situation is the same: few women in the most senior posts. For example, in the Salvation Army half the officers are women, but only about 10 per cent of those in senior leadership positions are women.

In the Church of England the number of women clergy in 2002 was 2539, 20 per cent of the total; by 2006, it was around 3000. The percentage of women being ordained each year is increasing. In 1995 there were 44 women and 314 men priested. In 2006, it was 244 women and 234 men: parity was reached.

But the picture is rather different when we look at how men and women are deployed. Out of those ordained deacon in 1993 (just after the vote to ordain women to the priesthood), 45 per cent of the men were incumbents by 2006, but only 18 per cent of the women (though 'incumbency status' posts such as priest in charge raise these percentages to 67 per cent and 45 per cent respectively). Women make up the majority of those in unpaid posts.

Differences are also emerging, in US and UK churches, in where women are deployed. In some areas, it is clear that more women are serving in tough inner-city or equally demanding rural groups of churches than in suburban ones. This repeats a pattern which I found in my research on women and church planting—that plants in middle-class places were often led by men, while women led plants in difficult places such as new housing areas or the inner city.

When it comes to senior posts, in 2005 there were 68 women

area deans (responsible for looking after an area of around 10–20 churches and their leaders) out of 697, and as at June 2007 there were 13 women archdeacons, 14 canons attached to cathedrals, two women deans and, of course, no bishops.

The patterns are similar in the USA. Women make up the majority of church members, yet leadership is still overwhelmingly male. In the last 20 years the number of women in church leadership has risen steadily, and women are now serving in positions not previously open to them, such as bishops. The US Episcopal Church now has twelve women bishops and women make up one third to one half of students in seminaries. But women are often paid less than men in the same positions and find it hard to move into senior posts. In black churches there are 2.5 to 3 women to each man in the congregations, yet women make up only about 5 per cent of clergy in the historic black denominations. In Asian churches women are usually the majority of worshippers but are marginalized in the power structure. Ninety per cent of senior pastors in Protestant churches are men, and the majority of denominational leadership is also male.

This is self-perpetuating: if women do not see themselves in leadership positions, they subconsciously assume that they should not and cannot lead. Women are beginning to move into senior posts in the Church of England. Some bishops want to appoint women to balance their leadership teams in dioceses. While some women have been appointed, there is also concern that some women who are invited to apply for such posts say 'no', while others who apply do not have the right experience. How can this logjam be broken?

There are two ways of approaching this issue: what needs to be done by bishops and other senior leaders to attract more women, and what women themselves can do. A report published in 2007, *Talent and Calling*,[16] includes recommendations for how the Church can better identify and develop those with leadership talent, particularly women and those from minority ethnic backgrounds, who are also under-represented in senior posts. Thus some solutions have begun to emerge, ranging from better application forms, which take account of non-ordained experience, to the possibility of providing women with wider experience through work shadowing or placements, and the need for women to engage more strategically, think about career development and be willing to be pioneers. The suggestions later in this chapter and in the Resource Section may help women who feel that God may be calling them to a senior post.

Women and larger churches

Why is it also true that relatively few women are appointed to larger churches? According to the 2005 church census, the largest church in England led by a woman had a congregation of 297. The situation is similar in the USA, although it appears that the situation is starting to change there—and, to some extent, in the UK. According to recent research on women in the (US) Episcopal Church, 'the larger the congregation, the less willing people are to have a woman as their rector'.[17] In the UK, an able and experienced woman priest applied to be vicar in a large evangelical church. Although she was told after the interview that she was the best candidate, the interviewers said that they could not bring themselves to appoint her. At some gut level she was seen as a risk. Molly Marshall, the first female president of a Baptist seminary, writes of the US Baptist scene, 'There's still a challenge in placement of women in positions of leadership... Women pastors are often called to smaller, less prestigious churches, or simply receive less pay than their male equivalents.'[18] However, in June 2007 a woman was appointed senior minister of First Baptist Church of Decatur, Alabama, a church of 2700 members, and this may well soon be followed by more.

One Anglican woman saw an advertisement for an associate minister post in a large evangelical church. She phoned up to ask for details and the administrator said that the church was not looking for a woman. This turned out to be a unilateral decision by the vicar, not even agreed by the church council. Many Anglican women have told me that it's harder in some ways to be an evangelical woman looking for a job than someone from the high church tradition. If churches have passed any of the Resolutions,[19] you know where you are, but evangelical churches can say that they are open to women—but not this time, or not yet. However, some leaders of larger evangelical churches are waking up to the fact that women often feel excluded.

Who knows what the future holds? We live in 'interesting times' in the Church, facing a variety of issues and pressures that may affect attitudes to women leaders in the future. While much has been achieved, there are still many challenges. I long to see those in denominations with the power to make changes acknowledging the gifts that women bring to leadership and the theological necessity to open up the leadership of the Church at every level to women serving alongside men.

How can women be more proactive in their own development as leaders? We will now turn to consider this question, as well as how mentoring can be a vital tool for women leaders.

FOLLOWING YOUR DREAMS: DEVELOPING AS A LEADER

What is your passion? Many writers on leadership see discovering and living by your passions as one key to a meaningful life. Women, like men, have dreams, but the only way to ensure that those dreams become reality is to do some planning. If vision is at the heart of leadership, vision involves not only seeing a picture of the future for our church or organization, but also seeing a picture of the future for ourselves. Finding a way of doing this is essential to anyone who is stepping up to leadership.

Being intentional

One observation sometimes made about women who are aspiring to leadership in a business or organization is that they are not as intentional as men are, and this is one reason why they fail to achieve the same level of leadership. The same, I suspect, may be true of Christian leaders. But why should we as Christians fail to be intentional about what we do? After all, God knows the plan for our lives even before we are born (Jeremiah 1:5); this does not mean that our lives are determined but it does suggest pattern and purpose. We can see in scripture that God has future leadership in mind for a person long before that person is aware of it. As Moses contemplated his strange life as a Hebrew in the Egyptian court, did he know that this experience was exactly what he would need in the future? As Mary learned the scriptures as a child, did she know that she would be chosen to be the mother of God's Son?

As women leaders, how do we find an appropriate balance between thinking we can dictate to God how our future will work out and letting our lives just drift by? Surely the latter is just as unhelpful as the former? Yet if our current leadership responsibilities are tough already, it's easy to muddle on, juggling work and domestic responsibilities and only occasionally being shaken up by a crisis that jolts us into learning new skills. For Christians, this is part of honouring who we are and being open to all that God wants to do through us. We need to take time to work with the big picture in mind, formulating a life plan and setting goals.

So how do women become more intentional about their lives and ministries? One way is through putting together a life vision, a summary of the person God has made them to be and the ways in which he may want them to use their personality, gifts and talents. There are plenty of materials around to help them to develop such a 'vision statement'. As we have already seen, women's lives are often more 'improvised' than men's, but that does not mean that they cannot have a sense of the end in mind.

One of the most effective ways I've found of focusing on what my future might look like, and how I might get there, is to imagine that I am writing about myself in ten years' time, as if I am describing someone else. It takes some effort to write in this way, and I only arrive at this stage after reading and praying through a number of themes.[20] Other ways might involve revisiting the earliest passions in our lives or our life story,[21] or starting a 'passion journal' and recording insights from God that will make our vision clearer. Much of this could well be done within a group rather than as an individual process, as we often know ourselves better when we see ourselves as others see us.

A life vision is simply a tool to help us identify God's priorities for our lives. It is not intended to set aside the Bible or to subvert grace as the starting point for understanding God's work in our lives. But it can act as a focus for the yearnings, dreams and aspirations, together with what we learn about our gifts and talents, that will enable us to make the most of who God has made us.

How has God SHAPEd you?

The first stage of this vision-discerning process may be to take stock of who we are. Many people have found that using the letters SHAPE from Rick Warren's *The Purpose-Driven Life*[22] helps to focus this exercise:

- **Spiritual gifts:** What God-empowered abilities do I have?
- **Heart:** What do I love to do? What do I care about most?
- **Abilities:** What are the things I can't help myself doing, the things I've always done well, my talents?
- **Personality:** What sort of person am I? (Do I enjoy people or tasks, routine or variety, action or reflection, and so on?)
- **Experience:** How have the events and experiences of my life shaped me so far?

As we explore and reflect on these aspects of our lives, patterns may emerge. How may these patterns project into the future? If it does not sound too depressing, can you imagine what you'd want someone to say about you in an obituary? How would you like to be remembered? What would you really like to achieve as God works through you and your ministry? A retreat or quiet day would provide a good opportunity to start drawing threads together.

How we capture these things in detail is up to us. It may be in a picture, a diagram, a list of bullet points or a poem. It should encompass the whole of life: who am I before God, and who does he want me to be, spiritually, relationally, professionally, personally, physically and recreationally?

The value of gaining some clarity is that it will help us with the big problem that all leaders face: prioritizing. What do we say 'yes' to and when should we say 'no'? It's much easier to say 'no' to this invitation or piece of work, however important it may seem, if we have a bigger 'yes' inside us, telling us that those are not our real priorities—but another invitation, another piece of work, is the one we should take on. This may make all the difference to our lives, even though it may be hard to do, especially if we are someone whose life has often revolved round saying 'yes' to others and 'no' to ourselves, our own dreams and aspirations.

Turning vision into living

As we think about the future and where we think God is leading us, how will we get there? Will we sit back, 'let go and let God', or will we be proactive? The whole subject of guidance is huge but I've always found it helpful to see it as 'both/and' rather than 'either/or'. It's not necessarily helpful to sit back and wait—which may be our default tendency as women.

Ultimately our lives are in God's hands—he is in control—but we are not meant to be passive. The saying that it's easier to steer a moving ship than a stationary one has often encouraged me to move ahead. We need to remember that God says, 'Whether you turn to the right or to the left, your ears will hear a voice behind you, saying, "This is the way; walk in it"' (Isaiah 30:21).

As we look to the future, what can we do to move towards it? Just as, in formulating the vision for a church, we might come up with a picture and some steps we would need to take to move towards it, so it is with a personal vision. We can break five-year goals down into goals for the next twelve months. A version of this exercise provides a useful tool for working towards particular areas of competence in our leadership role, or towards goals in our wider life. For example, we may be an assistant minister and know that when we step up to being sole leader we will have to chair many more meetings, but we don't feel we've mastered the skill yet. We can plan a learning strategy as follows:

Chairing meetings better

- How I am: some experience but lack confidence, especially keeping time, dealing with difficult people.
- How I want to be: more confident, a good enabling chairperson.
- Possible strategies: read up on chairing meetings, ask if I can act as chair in a new context, offer to chair evangelism committee, chat to a friend who does it well, talk to my mentor.
- Best option(s): some reading, plus gain safe experience, coupled with feedback and an opportunity to talk it through with mentor.
- Action: put times in my diary to make these things happen.

Or it may be that we know we don't eat very well and we would like to feel fitter. Our strategy might look like this:

Healthy eating

- How I am: eating unhealthily, often rushing, answering the phone while eating or skipping meals and eating after evening meetings; don't have time to cook properly.

- How I want to be: eating more healthy meals at the proper time.
- Possible strategies: use answerphone during meals, eat main meal at lunch time, cook in quantity and freeze in portions for later, plan some meetings around unhurried meals, keep healthy snacks such as bananas rather than crisps and chocolate.
- Best options: answerphone, cook ahead, buy fruit.
- Action: write a note to remind myself about answerphone, buy fruit, make a list of six meals that I can cook ahead, work out quantities needed and buy some small freezer tubs to store. Get in the habit of cooking one of these dishes each week.

The following list may help us to identify areas of leadership where we want to grow:

- Time management: planning and prioritizing.
- Emotional intelligence: self-awareness, relational skills.
- Leading teams: identifying team members, motivating, operating as team.
- Dealing with change and conflict: vision, change management.
- Work–life balance: prioritizing, support networks, exercise.

How could you develop? While most church structures are not very proactive in helping leaders develop beyond the earliest stages of professional ministry, there is no reason why you should not take the initiative—and, if you value who God has made you to be, it can be the best way forward. There is an additional checklist on developing as a leader in the Resource Section.

MENTORING

Writers on women in leadership emphasize the importance of networks and support structures. In particular, in a professional context, mentoring is seen as a key tool for developing leadership skills and progressing in an organization; a mentor can provide feedback, resources and access to the power structures of the organization. Many women feel that they are expected to be someone else, and struggle to be themselves. For some, 'mentoring provides a place that welcomes women to come as they are. At its best, mentoring is a process that beckons to women and encourages them to lower their masks'.[23]

In a church context, mentoring is increasingly possible as a tool in discipleship, but it can also help women who are stepping up to leadership. Women sometimes struggle to establish an identity as a leader, to understand church politics and power, to find support, and mentoring can be helpful in all these areas. One woman who was about to move up from an assistant post to the role of church leader told me, 'Top of my wish list for help as a leader is—a mentor.'

What is mentoring?

Over the last few years, mentoring has become a 'buzz' word in the world of work, as well as in church circles. It is a much talked about and much written about topic. But what is it? Mentoring is commonly a relationship where one person (normally more experienced, or senior, or with particular skills or wisdom to impart) seeks to guide the life of another with the aim of personal or professional growth, by mutual agreement. There are also other models: *peer mentoring*, an equal relationship between two people, and *group mentoring*, where three or four people meet and take it in turns to give each other time and attention. A specific form of group mentoring, useful for some contexts, is the use of Action Learning Sets. These involve a group of people (4–6) who commit to meeting and taking it in turns to present an issue to the rest of the group, who then help the presenter to work on it.[24]

Christian mentoring: a definition

There are many definitions of mentoring, but the following is used in the Arrow Leadership Programme (www.cpas.org.uk/arrow), and draws on other definitions:

Christian mentoring is a dynamic, intentional relationship of trust, in which one person (mentor) enables another (mentee or mentoree) to maximize the grace of God in their life, through the Holy Spirit, in the service of God's kingdom purposes, by sharing their life, experiencee and resources.

If these ideas and terms are new, we may be more familiar in a church context with 'spiritual director,' 'counsellor' and 'work consultant'. Again, these can be defined in various ways.

- 'Spiritual direction' is mainly concerned with the spiritual life: your relationship with God and how that is worked out in your life. People usually meet with a spiritual director every two or three months, over a number of years.
- 'Counselling' focuses on solving a particular problem, and usually takes place fairly intensively (weekly), over a short time, until the crisis is resolved or situation eased.
- A 'work consultant' is someone whose role is to help you to think through, review and analyse work issues. Like mentoring, consultancy is more about asking good questions than giving advice, but both work consultants and mentors will ideally have expertise on which they can draw to help you.

For a Christian, 'all biblical mentoring is under-mentoring. Jesus Christ is the real and decisive agent in Christian mentoring. We cannot bring about change in our mentorees, yet we can influence them to be changed by Jesus Christ'.[25] There is a wealth of resources on mentoring, both from a general and a specifically Christian perspective. Some are suggested in the Resource Section at the end of the book.

Mentoring for women leaders

If we believe that God is calling us to use our leadership gifts within the wider Church or in a senior post, we may look for a mentor within the church hierarchy who can help us in particular ways. As I look back on my first few years in ordained ministry, I can see a number of people who helped me in a mentoring type relationship. Some of them took time to give me leadership opportunities; in other cases they were people whom I sought out when I needed help.

Most of my mentors have been men. Over the last 20 or 30 years, as women have aspired to senior posts in the corporate world and the professions, women have often looked to men to mentor them, as they were already doing the jobs, had the necessary experience, and knew what was needed to help women to progress.

Now, in the next generation, women in business usually look to other women to mentor them. Many women have found that having another woman as mentor allows them to be themselves much more readily. A woman mentor may be able to provide particular insights, such as an insider's reading on the male/female culture of your work situation, and offer support as you develop your own effective style.

Women tend to bring a more holistic view to mentoring. One of the biggest stress points for many women in leadership is juggling the responsibilities of their work with home and possibly children, and other women will find it easier to understand this than many men can. Women are also likely to put more emphasis on collaboration than on hierarchy, and more emphasis on exchanging than on bestowing wisdom.

I have mentored a number of women but, in the past, I have usually preferred to do this fairly informally, even if I have met with my mentee at a set time each month or at whatever interval we have agreed. At one time I used to take people for walks by the canal, or through a big park, near the city where I lived: I found it easier to talk while walking than sitting down, and it felt less intense. On another occasion, 'mentoring' took place during car journeys to a training course, when I was getting a lift with one of the students. She was finding her feet in ministry and during the journey she was able to explore many issues and bounce ideas off someone outside her church context.

Some issues that may be of particular concern to women leaders are:

- Coping with discrimination, open or hidden.
- Wrestling with the question, 'What does it mean to be a woman in ministry?'
- Feeling that collaborative skills are unrecognized and unrewarded.
- Being excluded from informal networks.
- Lack of role models.
- Lack of a clear 'road map' for being a successful woman leader (or any kind of leader).
- Competing expectations, juggling home and work responsibilities, church cultural pressure to conform to stereotypes.
- Handling ambition.
- Handling positive and negative feedback.
- How to demonstrate vulnerability appropriately.
- Coping with loneliness—in ministry, at home, or both.
- How to demonstrate appropriate assertiveness.

Here are some comments from women leaders about the experience of being mentored:

'My mentor helps me to reflect on how God is working in and through me.'

'My mentoring relationship is fantastic! It's wonderful to have the chance to think out loud with someone incredibly wise and insightful.'

'She's a careful listener and asks good questions and therefore makes me think and reflect.'

Cross-gender mentoring

The lack of women leaders at senior levels in Christian circles, and lack of women who have been mentored themselves, means that it is hard for some women to find a woman who is 'further ahead' to be a mentor. As one woman in senior leadership writes:

There are some wonderful women with very humble, Christ-like maturity and wisdom in the Church, but very few in the generation above me who have 'got' (if I can express it that way) serving and living as a leader in the church. They therefore have had little understanding and experience that I could draw upon.[26]

Another woman leader notes that most of her mentors have been male but she now has a female mentor. She suggests that we can do cross-gender mentoring so long as we are wise; it is often seen as the norm in a secular context. And even when numbers of male and female leaders are much more equal, there will still be value in cross-gender mentoring. While, at present, women may particularly value being mentored by other women, the last thing we need is for women to find support only in same-sex groups. In order to work against the division between the sexes, women and men need to learn and grow together.

For cross-gender mentoring, it is sensible to agree on some guidelines:

- Clearly define the relationship and expectations.
- Meet in a public place, or somewhere where there are others known to you around. Avoid situations that could be interpreted as compromising.
- The mentor and mentee should both inform their spouses (if they are married) or other close Christian friends of their mentoring relationship, and should each be accountable to someone of their own sex.

- Consider bringing the topics discussed to prayer with a different person; manage the boundaries of intimacy with wisdom.

And finally

If you think you would benefit from mentoring to help you to become a better leader, go for it! It's up to those who want to be mentored to make the running. You may find that mentoring can arise out of an existing friendship, or you may want to be more intentional, or ask someone you think would be good. Don't be shy: if you don't ask, they can't say yes![27]

Robyn Claydon, who for many years has been mentoring women who are leaders in evangelism, writes this:

Mentoring is rather like running an Olympic relay race. The older, more experienced leaders running the Christian race are—or will be—in the process of handing the baton on to those coming up behind. They don't suddenly hand the baton on, for the other person may not be ready and drop it. For a time, as in the race, one runs alongside the other, giving him or her strength and encouragement and handing on the baton when they know they are ready.

Mentoring is running alongside someone else for as long as it takes.[28]

SIGNS OF HOPE

All these things will help women to step up to leadership and take their place alongside men. To overcome centuries of patriarchy is an uphill struggle, but once we realize that God's intention is for men and women to lead together, we must work to change the culture, starting with the Church. Here the aim is a balance of male and female in leadership, whether in churches, dioceses, denominational leadership or leadership of parachurch organizations. This in turn will help to create a climate where women are free to develop their leadership gifts and will no longer get the message 'Women don't do this.'

There are many signs of hope. One woman, Kelly, has written about how she struggled to find her place amid the male-dominated 'emerging church' movement in the USA. She went to a conference and found herself one of only two women among 150 men: 'Because of the evangelical heritage of much of the emerging church, cultural shifts need to be made to make way for women to minister as co-equals.' Encouraged by some of the male leaders, a group of women got together to empower other women and to make a difference in the 'emerging' community.

For Kelly, this has been an exciting journey. From being silenced as a leader in a church where only men could be pastors and elders, 'I have found a place that I can come along and make a difference, a place where my leadership style is recognized, a place where there is room for difference and room for questions, a place where I can practice new ways of being a leader with permission.'[29]

QUESTIONS FOR REFLECTION AND DISCUSSION

- What one thing are you going to do as a result of reading this chapter?
- How can you make the most of how God has made you and what he has given you?
- Reflect on the kind of helper that you would most value at the moment: mentor/coach/spiritual director/work consultant. Then find one!
- What changes could you make in your church so that girls and young women receive the message that women can be leaders? Can you make those changes or identify what is stopping you from making them?

- If you have some experience as a leader, identify an emerging young leader and pray for her. How could you encourage and support her as she develops?

✣

CONCLUSION

'*The dialogue on women and leadership in the church is oceanic in scope, and the truth is that you could easily drown in the discussion. Many have. Some have treaded water for years and are just emerging from the tide, a bit worn out, but full of anticipation to find both feet on solid ground. Now that our legs are strong we are ready to run, hard and fast towards becoming who we already are in Christ and using our leadership gifts in and for the Kingdom.*'[1]

Many women find the Church a confusing and challenging place to be a leader. 'Tomorrow belongs to women,' cry the leadership experts, but most women see little sign of that in the Church. In any case, tomorrow belongs to God, and, I believe, to a shared leadership of women and men.

This book has explored some of the challenges that women leaders have faced in the past and still face today, in living out their calling. Starting with the assumption that the Bible is the word of God, but must be correctly interpreted and seen in its cultural context, I have concluded that there is no convincing case for denying that women should be leaders in the Church. In addition, we have seen that women have moved into leadership in many areas of life and are now accepted as competent and capable leaders.

A RADICAL DIAGNOSIS

However we interpret the events of Genesis 3, they have affected life ever since. The Fall resulted in men's tendency to dominate women, which resulted in what we call 'patriarchy'. At the same time, women have tended to put the preservation of relationship above their God-given task of using their gifts. Human beings were alienated from God and from each other, but Jesus came to change all that. On the cross he set us free not only from the sin we individually commit, but also from the wider effects of the Fall, including women's and men's alienation from each other.

From the time of Jesus, we see the beginnings of that new order. As Jesus died, his women disciples were with him to the end, and he entrusted the greatest message ever delivered—news of his resurrection—to a woman. From Pentecost onwards, we see women playing their part alongside men in the communities of Christians that began to spring up around the Roman Empire. But radical views of women's equality were not easily accepted. Through the last 2000 years, short periods of gift-based ministry, in which women were able to play a full part in Christian ministry and lead alongside men, were followed by male-led institutionalization and rules about who could do what in God's Church. Often women were relegated to the sidelines, but sought to continue to use their gifts, all the while longing for a return to God's ideal, a world in which men and women work together.

All this time, the Church has missed being a shop window to the world of how God intends human relationships to be. It has missed the opportunity to encourage all God's people to discover who he made them to be and to use their gifts fully. Imbibing ideas from the culture around it, the early Church instead decreed that women and men should be treated differently, a legacy that still plays itself out in the lives of countless women and girls today.

Women's exclusion from leadership in the Church is part of the spiritual battle. Woman was designed to be an equal partner with man in God's great salvation story, but the denial of this allowed Satan to attack the pinnacle of God's creation, men and women, and to attack God himself. Our ancient foe has kept men and women behaving like fallen men and women, not like post-Pentecost men and women. Many women have been silenced, removed from the spiritual workforce. Many men, believing that women are not equal to men, have succumbed to the sin of pride. And the message that many inside and outside the Church have heard is that God is unjust.

Thus it is not enough to say, as some Christians have done, that justice demands that women should be leaders. It is just a matter of time, they say, before all Christians will come to accept it. We do not need to worry about these arguments; just demonstrate that women can do the job, and the problem will be solved. Some women leaders feel that being a leader is demanding enough. Why get involved in these greater theological issues? But if this issue is not just cultural but spiritual, a more radical solution is needed. I have already drawn parallels between slavery and the oppression of women. As I have listened in the past few years to discussion about the slave trade and possible apologies and compensation, I have wondered, will Christian women, will women in general, ever receive an apology?

Our society now treats men and women as equals (more or less). Discrimination against someone on the grounds of race, taken for granted only a couple of hundred years ago, is now (rightly) a criminal offence. Are the issues about women as leaders really about a few scriptures that many theologians still struggle to understand? Or are they more about power and control, about prejudice, pride and the protection of privilege? If so, the only way to break the power of this sin is for those who have withheld leadership from women to repent, to ask for forgiveness, and to seek to create a better future. Where women have neglected their gifts, failing to develop and use the leadership gifts that God has given them, they may be guilty too, and may need to repent to break the power of sin over them.

A NEW FUTURE?

One writer on women's leadership (not a Christian) puts it like this. She contrasts the Warrior, the traditional male hero who charges into battle with the aim of dominating and winning, with the Martyr, the female heroic archetype whose central tasks are care, sacrifice and redemptive suffering. She explores how these two cultures are coming together, and proposes the image of Magician for the figure who unites them. The Magician knows how to sacrifice without losing personal identity, and how to work hard to achieve without succumbing to a competitive struggle. At this level dualities break down. The Magician is characterized by receptiveness, tapping into and drawing strength from energy sources outside him- or herself. As Christians we already look to such a person, one whose 'magic deeper still' (in the words of Aslan) transformed our world. His name is Jesus.

And this is, finally, what we should expect as Christians trying to define the essence of Christian leadership. As we have seen, it is almost impossible to define the 'essence' of being male or female, yet we know that we exist in two kinds and that we can make some very broad generalizations about our differences. There is something about the nature of God that is reflected in maleness and femaleness *together*, not in being a male or female separately, or being more male than female. Humanness is the combination of maleness and femaleness. Thus ideal leadership is in this togetherness, which also consists of a unique blend of experience and personality that women and men together offer the Church.

At least in the West, we seem to be inching towards a more collaborative society, a culture in which the merits of both sexes are understood, valued and employed. We have to wait for the full healing of all relationships. I believe that the 21st century may be the first to see the sexes live and work as equals—the way men and women were designed to live. I long for God's Church to lead the way, as it started to do 2000 years ago. The gender wars began in Eden but ended at Calvary. When women's and men's voices are heard and valued at all levels, we may get nearer to creating churches—and communities—that are places of mutual trust, connected intimacy and shared power.

I HAVE A DREAM...

I dream of a church
where women and men work together
in leadership and evangelism;

Where women use their gifts,
discover new ones,
and empower other men and women;

Where men and women
are seen as fellow-workers together
and fellow-servants of each other.

I dream of a church
which is seen by outsiders
as one where women are affirmed,
encouraged and fulfilled
in their God-given callings;

Where men and women working together
reflect the image of God,
and, in Christ,
overcome the 'battle of the sexes'.

I dream of a church
which proclaims to women and men
the good news of true liberation in Christ.

✛

RESOURCE SECTION

The following resources are listed by chapter. I do not necessarily agree with all the content of the books, but they are all worth reading. Not all are available in bookshops, but all should be obtainable via book-ordering services. Website details were correct at the time of writing.

www.cpas.org.uk/womeninleadership: this is a website area devoted to women in leadership, with a variety of articles, book reviews and other resources covering all the areas in this book.

Part 1: Women as leaders

Chapter 1

Linda L. Belleville, *Women Leaders and the Church: Three Crucial Questions*, Baker Books, 2000

Loren Cunningham and David Hamilton, *Why not Women? A Biblical Study of Women in Missions, Ministry and Leadership*, YWAM Publishing, 2000

Ruth B. Edwards, *The Case for Women's Ministry*, SPCK, 1989

Kevin Giles, *The Trinity and Subordinationism: the Doctrine of the Trinity and the Contemporary Gender Debate*, IVP, 2002

Ronald W. Pierce and Rebecca Merrill Groothuis (eds.), *Discovering Biblical Equality: Complementarity without Hierarchy*, IVP, 2005

John Stackhouse, *Finally Feminist*, Baker Academic, 2005

Sarah Sumner, *Men and Women in the Church: Building Consensus on Christian Leadership*, IVP, 2003

www.cbeinternational.org: A source of theological and practical articles from a biblical equality perspective.

Chapter 2

Eldon Jay Epp, *Junia: The First Woman Apostle*, Fortress Press, 2005

Mary Evans, *Woman in the Bible*, Paternoster Press, 1983

Carolyn Custis James, *Lost Women of the Bible*, Zondervan, 2005

Kevin Madigan and Carolyn Osiek (eds.), *Ordained Women in the Early Church: a Documentary History*, The Johns Hopkins University Press, 2005

Carolyn Osiek and Margaret Y. MacDonald, *A Woman's Place: House Churches in Earliest Christianity*, Fortress Press, 2006

Chapter 3

Laura Swan, *The Forgotten Desert Mothers*, Paulist Press, 2001

Ruth A. Tucker and Walter W. Liefeld, *Daughters of the Church: Women and Ministry from New Testament Times to the Present*, Zondervan, 1987

Paul Chilcote, *She Offered Them Christ: the Legacy of Women Preachers in Early Methodism*, Abingdon Press, 1993

Diana Chapman, *Searching the Source of the River: Forgotten Women of the British Pentecostal Revival 1907–1914*, PUSH Publishing, 2007

Valerie Griffiths, *Not Less than Everything: the Courageous Women who Carried the Christian Gospel to China*, Monarch, 2004

Part 2: Ways women lead

Chapter 4

Jim Collins, *Good to Great,* Random House, 2001

Eddie Gibbs, *Leadership Next*, IVP, 2005

Daniel Goleman, *The New Leaders*, Time Warner Paperbacks, 2003

James Lawrence, *Growing Leaders,* BRF, 2004

Henri Nouwen, *In the Name of Jesus*, DLT, 1989

David Robertson, *Collaborative Leadership*, BRF, 2007

Andy Stanley, *Next Generation Leader: 5 Essentials for Those who Will Shape the Future,* Multnomah, 2006

Margaret Wheatley, *Leadership and the New Science: Discovering Order in a Chaotic World,* Berrett-Koehler, 1999

Walter Wright, *Relational Leadership*, Paternoster, 2000

www.teal.org.uk: Christian Leadership World, a site with a variety of resources on leadership

Chapter 5

Deborah Cameron, *The Myth of Mars and Venus*, OUP, 2007

Alice H. Eagly and Linda L. Carli, *Through the Labyrinth: the Truth about How Women Become Leaders*, Harvard Business School Press, 2007

Sally Helgesen, *The Female Advantage: Women's Ways of Leadership*, Doubleday, 1990 (paperback edition 1995)

Sally Helgesen, *The Web of Inclusion: a New Architecture for Building Great Organizations*, Doubleday, 1995

Jeanne Porter, *Leading Ladies: Transformative Biblical Images for Women's Leadership*, Innisfree Press, 2000

Elaine Storkey, *Created or Constructed? The Great Gender Debate*, Paternoster, 2000

Mary Stewart van Leeuwen, *Gender and Grace: Women and Men in a Changing World*, IVP, 1990

Susan Willhauck, *Backtalk! Women Leaders Changing the Church*, Pilgrim Press, 2005

Part 3: Issues women face

Dan Allender, *To Be Told: Know Your Story, Shape Your Future*, WaterBrook, 2005

Julie Baker, *A Pebble in the Pond: Leadership Skills Every Woman Can Achieve*, Cook Communications, 2001

Katie Brazelton, *Praying for Purpose for Women*, Zondervan, 2005

Marcus Buckingham, *Go Put Your Strengths to Work*, Simon & Schuster UK, 2007

Marcus Buckingham and Donald O. Clifton, *Now, Discover Your Strengths*, Simon & Schuster UK, 2004

Stephen Covey, *The Seven Habits of Highly Effective People*, Summit Books, 1989

Nick Helm and Philip Allin (eds.), *Finding Support in Ministry*, Grove P90, 2002

Bryn Hughes, *Discipling, Coaching, Mentoring*, Kingsway, 2003

Emma Ineson, *Busy Christian Living: Blessing Not Burden*, Continuum, 2007

Nadine Kazerounian, *Stepping Up: Women's Guide to Career Development,* McGraw-Hill, 2002

Carson Pue, *Mentoring Leaders: Wisdom for Developing Character, Call and Competency*, Baker, 2005

Tom Rath, *StrengthsFinder 2.0*, Gallup Press, 2007

Andrew Seidel, *Charting a Bold Course*, Moody, 2006

Paul D. Stanley and Robert Clinton, *Connecting*, Navpress, 1992

Sarah Sumner, *Leadership Above the Line*, Tyndale, 2006

Peninah Thomson and Jacey Graham, *A Woman's Place is in the Board Room,* Palgrave Macmillan, 2005

Rick Warren, *The Purpose-Driven Life*, Zondervan, 2002

DEVELOPING SELF-AWARENESS

One way to develop as a leader is by developing in self-awareness, including an understanding of our gifts, talents, how we are perceived by others, and so on. Listed below are brief introductions to a number of tools, with information on how to obtain and use them.

Spiritual gifts

Essential for a Christian leader is an awareness of our spiritual gifts. Gifts are given to every believer (1 Corinthians 7:7), irrespective of their age or their maturity as a Christian. Often we will become aware of our gifts as we grow in our faith and listen to others. We need to ask God to show us what our gifts are, and be prayerful as we explore them. Most of the gifts are listed in three passages in the Bible: 1 Corinthians 12:8–10, Romans 12:6–8 and Ephesians 4:11.

There are lists and descriptions of gifts in a number of books—the descriptions varying according to the theology of the author.

Graham Cray, *Tools for the Job* (CPAS, 1990), is a practical workbook to use with groups within a church or organization. No longer in print but worth borrowing from someone.

The Willow Creek *Network Course,* designed to help church members discover their place of ministry in their local church, is available from the Willow Creek Association UK at www.willowcreek.org.uk. Also see a related book: *What You Do Best in the Body of Christ*, by Bruce Bugbee (Zondervan/Willow Creek, 1995), which covers passion, spiritual gifts and personal style.

A Spiritual Gifts Diagnostic Inventory is available from Lead Consulting, Raleigh, North Carolina, USA, www.leadconsulting-usa. com/pr01.htm. This explores gifts by experience and traits.

Jane Kise, David Stark and Sandra Krebs Hirsh, *Discover Who You Are: Why You're Here, What You Do Best (Lifekeys),* Bethany House, 2005. This book integrates the Myers-Briggs Type Indicator® with some other resources to help you identify gifts and passions.

Aubrey Malphurs, *Maximizing Your Effectiveness: How to Discover and Develop Your Divine Design,* Baker Books, 2006. Considers a whole range of elements including spiritual gifts.

Peter Wagner, *Your Spiritual Gifts Can Help Your Church Grow*, Regal Books, 2005.

You can access an online tool to identify your spiritual gifts at:

- www.buildingchurch.net/g2s.htm
- www.churchgrowth.org/cgi-cg/gifts.cgi

Talents

The latest version of the Gallup StrengthsFinder tool is available online by buying *StrengthsFinder 2.0* by Tom Rath. The book *Now, Discover Your Strengths* gives access to the earlier version, which is still extremely valuable.

Based on thousands of interviews, StrengthsFinder will give you a list of your top five 'themes' (talents), out of a list of 34. It is called 'StrengthsFinder' because the ultimate goal is to build on these talents so that they become strengths. The books also explain the thinking behind these tools, including the insight that it is more useful to focus on building on talents than on trying to correct weaknesses.

Myers-Briggs®

The Myers-Briggs Type Indicator® (MBTI) is a personality questionnaire designed to identify certain psychological differences according to the typological theories of Jung. The original developers of the indicator were Katharine Cook Briggs and her daughter, Isabel Briggs Myers, hence the name.

In a similar way to being left- or right-handed, the principle is that individuals find certain ways of thinking and acting easier than others. The MBTI endeavours to sort some of these psychological opposites into four pairs, with a resulting 16 possible combinations. Briggs and Myers recognized that everyone has an overall combination which is most comfortable for them: in the same way as writing with the left hand is hard work for a right-hander, so people tend to find using their opposite psychological preference more difficult, even if they can become more proficient (and therefore behaviourally flexible) with practice and development.

The personality types are notated with the initial letters of each of their four preferences, for instance:

ISTJ: Introverted, Sensing, Thinking, Judging
ENFP: Extraverted, iNtuitive, Feeling, Perceiving

The best way to discover your Myers-Briggs preferences is to go on a Myers-Briggs day or weekend; these are sometimes run at retreat houses. You will be asked to answer a series of questions, the responses are analysed, and you then find out how to interpret and work with your preferences.

Learning styles

A learning style is a preference for a way of learning. There are a variety of ways of considering these, and the four most common are:

- Kolb's learning style, which relates to Kolb's learning cycle (experience, reflection, decision, doing): www.businessballs.com
- Honey and Mumford's four styles (activist, pragmatist, reflector, theorist): www.peterhoney.com/content/tools-learningstyles.html
- Memletic seven styles (visual, social, physical, aural, verbal, solitary, logical): www.learning-styles-online.com
- VAK (visual, auditory, kinaesthetic): www.businessballs.com

The websites give further information and downloadable questionnaires (some free).

This is another area where it isn't a matter of right or wrong, just being different. A basic understanding of our learning style can help us to:

- tailor learning to our own preference to ensure we learn most effectively.
- understand why other people learn in different ways and therefore help create a healthy learning environment.
- work at our own communication to help a wide variety of people learn.

Also see:

Marlene LeFever, *Learning Styles*, Kingsway Communications, 1998

R. Dunn and K. Dunn, *The Complete Guide to the Learning Styles Inservice System*, Prentice Hall, 1998

www.engr.ncsu.edu/learningstyles

The dark side of leadership

Many traits that drive leaders to succeed also have the potential to bring out the 'dark side' of leadership. The book *Overcoming the Dark Side of Leadership* by Gary McIntosh and Samuel Rima (Baker Books, 1997) explores a variety of personal dysfunctions which can result in depression and burn-out or various kinds of destructive behaviour. The dark side produces the 'compulsive' leader, 'narcissistic' leader, 'paranoid' leader, 'codependent' leader and 'passive-aggressive' leader; each of these is explored in the book and there are inventories to help the reader identify their own 'dark side'. The book is predominantly 'male', but I am not aware of anything similar written by women and it contains useful insights.

Finally, here are two resources for use by teams:

Team roles

A tool commonly used to help people discover the roles they play in a team is Belbin® Team Roles. This is derived from research written up in the book *Management Teams—Why They Succeed or Fail* by Dr Meredith Belbin (latest edition: Butterworth-Heinemann, 1996). A team role is defined as 'Our tendency to behave, contribute and interrelate with others in a particular way'.

The tool can be self-scored from the book or via a trained consultant. It provides non-confrontational and non-hierarchical language to describe a person's natural behavioural preferences. There are nine team roles: Plant, Resource Investigator, Co-ordinator, Shaper, Monitor Evaluator, Teamworker, Implementer, Completer Finisher, Specialist. Further information is available on www.belbin.com.

The five dysfunctions of a team

The book by Patrick Lencioni, *The Five Dysfunctions of a Team: a Leadership Fable*, (Jossey-Bass, 2002), despite its negative-sounding title, is an excellent introduction to what makes team work well—or badly. Through a 'leadership fable' Lencioni reveals the five dysfunctions that go to the heart of why teams often struggle: absence of trust; fear of conflict; lack of commitment; avoidance of accountability; inattention to results. He outlines a model and action steps that can be used to overcome these issues. The book includes a simple diagnostic tool to help teams discover their weaknesses and then address them. While the book is based on work with CEOs and their executive teams, its theories are applicable to any teams, and the tool has been used in a variety of church contexts.

DEVELOPING AS A LEADER

Below is a checklist of ideas to help leaders focus on their development. Some denominations are moving towards a point where ministers will be expected to have certain competencies at different stages of their formation and for different roles. Having a list of competencies set out may help a leader to think ahead: what competencies might I need for my next role or the kind of ministry that God is calling me to? What are my weaknesses? While strengths-based thinking tells us to build on our strengths and manage our weaknesses, God will often call us to roles where we will use our strengths and but also have to do things that challenge our competency. Working in a leadership team will help this, but there are times when as leaders we have the ultimate responsibility.

What do I need to do to develop as a leader?

- First, pray: ask God to help you to grow.
- Find out what your talents and gifts are (if you don't know).
- Go to conferences, find additional training—for example, a leadership programme.[1]
- Find a mentor, work consultant, coach or spiritual director.
- Join or start a support network.[2]
- Volunteer for a role in the wider church—a committee, a role within a committee, a project or a parachurch organization that harnesses your passion. All these roles need to be taken on within the limits of your job, but I have found that churches and colleagues are supportive when they see that outside involvements benefit you (give you energy) and the church (a wider view of things, new ideas).
- Make time to read: 'leaders are readers'. Carve out time to read for, say, one hour a week and make a list of books you want to read (see the resources listed above).
- Listen to CDs and downloads (as you drive around your ministry area, do ironing, take the dog for a walk, or whatever).
- Be alert to new opportunities to learn, develop and progress. Treat difficulties and challenges as learning experiences.
- Constantly update your CV and think about possible gaps when it comes to relevant experience for your next post.
- Use ministerial reviews to articulate what, under God, you have accomplished, and something of your aspirations and training needs.
- Reflect on where you are getting stuck (at the stained-glass ceiling or in any aspect of leadership), and find someone to talk to about it.

- Spend time around great leaders; leadership is caught as much as it is taught.
- Pray about what you can do to be a good role model for other women and how you can develop other leaders.

The Church Pastoral Aid Society is an evangelical Anglican mission agency working mainly with local churches across the United Kingdom and the Republic of Ireland.

CPAS exists to inspire and enable churches to reach everyone in their communities with the good news of Jesus.

CPAS
Athena Drive
Tachbrook Park
WARWICK
CV34 6NG
01926 458458
info@cpas.org.uk
www.cpas.org.uk

The Arrow Leadership Programme aims to develop Christian leaders for the Church of the 21st century. It is not merely another course or conference—its aim is 'life transformation'. Over 18 months, Arrow helps participants to grow through teaching, reflection, worship, interaction, application, accountability and fun.

For further information visit www.cpas.org.uk/arrow or call CPAS.

NOTES

Introduction

1 Letty Russell, *Church in the Round*, Westminster/John Knox Press, 1993.

2 Dorothy R. Pape, *In Search of God's Ideal Woman: A Personal Examination of the New Testament*, Inter-Varsity Press, 1975.

3 Audrey Malphurs, quoted in Michael Quicke, *360-Degree Leadership*, Baker Books, 2006, p. 77.

4 Leanne Friesen, 'How are we doing? The continued plight of women and girls seeking leadership in Christian Churches', thesis at McMaster, Canada, 1995, pp. 19–21.

Chapter 1: Interpreting scripture

1 Sarah Sumner, *Men and Women in the Church*, IVP, 2003, p. 265.

2 Quoted in Christina Rees (ed.), *Voices of This Calling*, Canterbury Press, 2002, p. 63.

3 R.C. Ortland, 'Male–female equality and male headship' in Wayne Grudem and John Piper (eds.), *Recovering Biblical Manhood and Womanhood*, Crossway, 1991, p. 102.

4 John Stackhouse, *Finally Feminist*, Baker Academic, 2005, p. 75.

5 Tom Wright, 'The biblical basis for women's service in the Church', *Priscilla Papers* 20:4, pp. 5–6.

6 Howard Marshall, 'Lost in translation—inclusion in the Church', paper given at a Men Women and God conference, 7 October 2006.

7 John Stott, *The Message of 1 Timothy and Titus*, IVP, 1996, p. 74.

8 Linda L. Belleville, 'Teaching and usurping authority' in Ronald W. Pierce and Rebecca Merrill Groothuis (eds.), *Discovering Biblical Equality* (hereafter *DBE*), IVP, 2004, pp. 209–11.

9 Belleville, ibid. p. 219.

10 Ibid. p. 223.

11 Tom Wright, *Paul for Everyone: The Pastoral Letters*, SPCK, 2003, pp. 21–22.

12 Ibid. p. 25.

13 For a more detailed discussion of this verse, see Sarah Sumner, *Men and Women in the Church*, IVP, 2003, ch. 20.

14 Wright, *Paul for Everyone*, p. 25.

15 For the first of these, see, for example, Andrew Perriman, *Speaking of Women*, Apollos, 1998, p. 168; for the second, see John Stott, *The Message of 1 Timothy and Titus*, IVP, 1996, p. 87.

16 Quoted in Sumner, *Men and Women in the Church*, p. 41.

17 Elizabeth A. Clark, *Women in the Early Church*, Michael Glazier, 1983, p. 157.

18 Craig Keener, *Paul, Women and Wives*, Hendrickson, 1992.

19 'Learning in the Assemblies', *DBE*, ch. 9.

20 See Wright, 'The biblical basis for women's service in the Church'.

21 In full in Wayne Grudem, *Evangelical Feminism and Biblical Truth*, IVP, 2005, p. 537.

22 Alan Johnson, 'A meta-study of the debate over the meaning of "head" (*kephale*) in Paul's writings', *Priscilla Papers* 20:4, pp. 21–29.

23 Ibid. p. 25.

24 Grudem, *Evangelical Feminism and Biblical Truth*, IVP, 2005, p. 202.

25 Carolyn Osiek and Margaret Y. Macdonald, *A Woman's Place*, Augsberg Fortress, 2006.

26 (Zondervan, 2006.) Also see his earlier book, *The Trinity and Subordinationism: the Doctrine of the Trinity and the Contemporary Gender Debate,* IVP, 2002.

27 Phillip Cary, 'The new evangelical subordinationism: reading inequality into the Trinity' in *Priscilla Papers* 20:4, p. 42.

28 However one concludes the debate about head and source, any argument that requires a reordering of the text is debatable,

particularly when one is trying to prove a divine hand behind 'order'! See Gilbert Bilezikian, *Beyond Sex Roles*, Baker, 1985.

29 Giles, *The Trinity and Subordination*, p. 180.

30 For example, Leslie McFall in an unpublished book on the internet, *Good Order in the Church*, cites five signs of man's 'headship' in Genesis 2. Also see Wayne Grudem, *Evangelical Feminism and Biblical Truth*.

31 See, for example, footnote 28 in Stackhouse, *Finally Feminist*, p. 67.

32 McFall, *Good Order in the Church*.

33 See, for example, Rosy Ashley, 'Can a woman have authority over a man?' in Harriet Harris and Jane Shaw (eds.), *The Call for Women Bishops*, SPCK, 2004, pp. 89–93.

34 See, for example, Stackhouse, *Finally Feminist*, and Del Birkey, *The Fall of Patriarchy*, Fenestra Books, 2005.

35 Ed. Jonathan Baker (Canterbury Press, 2004).

36 Ibid. p. 50.

37 See Stackhouse, *Finally Feminist*, p. 80.

38 This interpretation comes from Frances Young, 'Hermeneutical Questions: the ordination of women in the light of biblical and patristic typology', unpublished paper, read at 'Women and Ordination in the Christian Churches: International Perspectives' 12–14 July 2006.

39 Lorry Lutz, *Women as Risk-Takers for God*, WEF Publications, 2000, p. 260.

Chapter 2: Leading women

1 Mary Evans, *Woman in the Bible*, Paternoster Press, 1983, p. 31.

2 To follow this line strictly, we would have to ask why leaders are not always Aramaic-speaking male Jews born in Galilee. At this time, women were believed to be inferior and even unclean: we only have to look at the way some male disciples responded to

the woman at the well (John 4:27) to see why there were limits to the way Jesus could challenge the culture of his day.

3 This label goes back to the third century at least, and was ascribed to her by the Church Fathers. It has been used by other commentators throughout Christian history: see Carolyn Custis James, *Lost Women of the Bible* (Zondervan, 2005), p. 238.

4 This is sometimes obscured by Bible translations that give a paragraph division, not present in the Greek, between verses 1 and 2.

5 Wright, 'The biblical basis for women's service in the Church', p. 7. Also see his *Luke for Everyone* (SPCK, 2001), p. 131, where he makes the same point.

6 Wright, 'The biblical basis for women's service in the Church', p. 7.

7 Ibid. p. 219.

8 See the book by Eldon Jay Epp, *Junia: the First Woman Apostle* (Fortress Press, 2005), which is devoted to this question.

9 Osiek and Macdonald, *A Woman's Place*, p. 9.

10 Ibid. p. 162.

11 Ibid. p. 25 and following; many other books have detailed discussions of Priscilla.

12 Kevin Madigan and Carolyn Osiek (eds.), *Ordained Women in the Early Church: A Documentary History*, Johns Hopkins University Press, 2005.

13 Ibid. pp. 113–14.

14 Ibid. p. 164.

15 Ibid. p. 9.

16 John Stackhouse, 'The use of history in evangelical gender debates', in Maxine Hancock (ed.), *Christian Perspectives on Gender, Sexuality and Community*, Regent College Publishing, 2003, p. 198.

17 Madigan and Osiek (eds.), *Ordained Women in the Early Church*, p. 205.

Chapter 3: Telling stories

1 A.J. Gordon, 'The ministry of women', *The Missionary View of the World*, 17 (1894), p. 914. Available online at www.cbeinternational.org/new/free_articles/ministry_of_women.pdf.
2 Jerome, *Epistle* 127.10.
3 Bede, *A History of the English Church and People*, Penguin, 1990, p. 244.
4 Margaret Ashton, *Lollards and Reformers*, The Hambledon Press, 1984, p. 60.
5 Margaret Fell, *Women's Speaking Justified*, 1666, Quaker Heritage Press Online Texts, no page number.
6 Paul W. Chilcote, *She Offered Them Christ*, Abingdon Press, 1993, p. 64.
7 Ibid. p. 40.
8 Mrs General Booth, *Female Ministry; Or Women's Right to Preach the Gospel*, The Salvation Army, 1909 edition, p. 3.
9 Ibid. p. 17.
10 Roger Green, 'Catherine Booth: model minister', *The War Cry*, 26 October 1996, p. 5.
11 Catherine Booth, 'Female ministry', in S.W. Partridge (ed.), *Papers on Practical Religion*, 1978, p. 123.
12 Frances Willard, *Woman in the Pulpit*, Lothrop, 1888 edn, p. 62.
13 From Thomas Blackburn, 'Luna', *Collected Poems*, Hutchinson, 1975.
14 Martin Robinson, endorsement to Diana Chapman's *Searching the Source of the River*, PUSH Publishing, 2007, p. iii.

Chapter 4: A brief history of leadership

1 Roberta Hestenes, 'Christian women and leadership', *Priscilla Papers*, 20:4 (2006), p. 32.

2 Margaret Wheatley, 'The servant-leader: from hero to host', an interview with Margaret Wheatley, 2002, www.margaretwheatley.com

3 The literature on leadership is vast. Some books are suggested in the Resource Section.

4 Marcus Buckingham and Donald Clifton, *Now, Discover Your Strengths*, Simon and Schuster, 2001, p. 48.

5 Access to this tool, StrengthsFinder 2.0, is through the book of that name by Tom Roth, Gallup, 2007.

6 Steven Croft, 'A theology of Christian leadership' in *Focus on Leadership,* Church Leadership Foundation, 2006, p. 13.

7 Ibid. p. 16.

8 Ibid. p. 17.

9 From the *Growing Leaders* course, written by James Lawrence and Simon Heathfield, published by CPAS, 2006.

10 Henri Nouwen, *In the Name of Jesus*, DLT, 1989, pp. 29–30.

11 Jim Collins, *Good to Great*, Random House, 2001, pp. 12–13.

12 Quoted in Susan Vinnicombe and John Banks, *Women with Attitude: Lessons in Career Management*, Routledge, 2003, p. 277.

13 Peter Senge, *The Fifth Discipline*, Doubleday, 1994, quoted in Leonard Hjalmarson, 'Kingdom leadership in the post-modern era', on the website Next Reformation, www.nextreformation.com, Winter, 2003.

14 Brian McLaren, 'Dorothy on leadership', *Rev. Magazine*, Nov/Dec 2000.

15 See Margaret Wheatley, *Leadership and the New Science*, Berrett-Koehler, 1999.

16 Hjalmarson, 'Kingdom leadership in the post-modern era', www.nextreformation.com.

17 See Jeanne Porter, *Leading Ladies*, Innisfree Press, 2000, ch. 1.

18 Hestenes, 'Christian women and leadership', pp. 31–35.

Chapter 5: Do women lead differently?

1   Susan Vinnicombe, 'What exactly are the differences in male and female working styles?' *Women in Management Review,* 1987.

2   Alice Eagly and Blair Johnson, 'Gender and leadership styles: a meta-analysis', *Psychological Bulletin*, 1990, 108:2, pp. 233–56.

3   Sally Helgesen, *The Female Advantage: Women's Ways of Leading*, Doubleday, 1995, pp. 159–60.

4   Helen Fisher, *The First Sex: The Natural Talents of Women and How they are Changing the World*, Ballantine, 1999, p. 288.

5   Leslie Francis, 'Male and female clergy in England: their personality differences, gender reversal?' *Journal of Empirical Theology*, 1992, 5, pp. 31–38.

6   Helen Thorne, *Journey to Priesthood*, monograph published by the University of Bristol, 2000.

7   For example, Anne Dyer, 'Reviewing the reception—five years of women priests', *Anvil* 16:2, p. 90.

8   Personal correspondence from a team rector.

9   'Leading with wisdom, compassion and patience, an interview with Molly Marshall', *Mutuality*, Spring 05, p. 5

10   Alice P. Mathews, *Preaching that Speaks to Women*, Baker, 2003, p. 132.

11   Hestenes, 'Christian women and leadership'.

12   Women quoted anonymously in Elizabeth Dyke, 'The stained glass ceiling', *The Church of England Newspaper*, 20 July 2007, p. 17.

13   Cited in Quicke, *360-Degree Leadership*, p. 147.

14   Bob Jackson, *The Road to Growth*, CHP, 2005, p. 43.

15   Ibid., p. 41.

16   Linda Coughlin, 'Introduction', in *Enlightened Power*, Linda Coughlin et al. (eds.), Jossey-Bass, 2005, p. 2.

Chapter 6: Power and service

1 Penny Jamieson, *Living at the Edge*, Mowbray, 1997, p. 26.
2 Robert Warren, quoted (without original source) in Philip King, *Leading a Church*, Administry, 1997, p. 4.
3 John Adair, quoted in Peter Shaw, *Mirroring Jesus as Leader*, Grove Books, 2004, p. 9.
4 Eddie Gibbs, *Leadership Next*, IVP, 2005, p. 23.
5 These are taken from Mathews, *Preaching that Speaks to Women*, p. 117.
6 Jamieson, *Living at the Edge*, p. 10.
7 Leighton Ford, *Transforming Leadership*, IVP, 1991, p. 76.
8 Personal correspondence to the author.
9 Joy Carroll, quoted in Michele Guinness, *Is God Good for Women?* Hodder, 1997, p. 225.
10 Janet Fife, in Rees (ed.), *Voices of This Calling*, p. 106.
11 Sue Hope, in Rees (ed.), *Voices of This Calling*, p. 199.
12 Mary Evans, quoted in 'There are no fences', *Mutuality*, Spring 2005, p. 28.
13 Nouwen, *In the Name of Jesus*, p. 63.

Chapter 7: Building confidence and courage

1 From 'Confessions of women in leadership', April 2006, www.soulsurvivor.com.
2 Quoted in Vinnicombe and Bank, *Women with Attitude*, p. 243.
3 Ibid., p. 243.
4 Helen Brown, 'Chocolate eclairs are not the answer', in the *Telegraph Review*, 7 October 2006, p. 29.
5 Helgesen, *The Female Advantage*, p. 163 (quoting Nancy Badore).
6 Marcus Buckingham, *The One Thing You Need to Know*, Simon and Schuster, 2005, p. 204.
7 Emily Vesey, quoted in 'Confessions of women in leadership', April 2006, www.soulsurvivor.com.

8 John Stott, *The Message of Romans*, IVP, 1994, p. 325.

9 Rosabeth Moss Kanter, *Confidence: how winning streaks and losing streaks begin and end* (Crown Business, 2004), p. 8.

10 These insights into Philippians are summarized from *The Dilemma of Self-Esteem* by Joanna and Alister McGrath, Crossway Books, ch. 7.

11 John Adair, *The Leadership of Jesus*, Canterbury Press, 2001, p. 178.

12 Shaw, *Mirroring Jesus as Leader*, p. 14.

13 Ibid.

14 Sandra Ford Walston, *Courage: the Heart and Spirit of Every Woman*, Broadway, 2002.

15 Ibid., p. 43.

16 Both stories from the July/August 2007 issue of *Barnabas Aid Magazine*, published by the Barnabas Fund.

17 These three expressions of courage (to say 'no', to face current reality and to dream) are drawn from Andy Stanley, *The Next Generation Leader,* Multnomah Publishers, 2003, ch. 6.

Chapter 8: Stepping up to lead

1 Quoted in Nadine Kazerounian, *Stepping Up*, McGraw-Hill, 2002, p. 93.

2 Tom Rath, *StrengthsFinder 2.0*, Gallup Press, 2007, p. 9.

3 Gretchen Englund in Carson Pue, *Mentoring Leaders*, Baker, 2005, p. 61.

4 *Revolve* New Testament, quoted in Friesen, 'How are we doing?' p. 23.

5 Joshua Harris, quoted in Friesen. p. 23.

6 Annie Flack, 'Digging deep: women in leadership', *Soul Survivor* magazine, on www.soulsurvivor.com, April 2006.

7 Buckingham, *The One Thing You Need to Know*, p. 238.

8 See Friesen, 'How are we doing?' pp. 35–38.

9   See Anna Fels, 'Do women lack ambition?' *Harvard Business Review*, April 2004.
10 Judith Rose, in Rees (ed.), *Voices of This Calling*, p. 39.
11 Mary Stewart van Leeuwen, *Gender and Grace*, IVP, 1990, p. 46.
12 *Letters of Theodore Dwight Weld, Angelina Grimke and Sarah Grimke, 1822–44*, quoted in Van Leeuwen, *Gender and Grace*, p. 59.
13 Deborah A. O'Neil and Diana Bilimora, 'Women's career development phases', *Career Development International*, 10:3, 2005, pp. 168–89.
14 Mary Catherine Bateson, quoted in Vinnicombe and Bank, *Women with Attitude*, p. xiv.
15 Sam Parkhouse, *Powerful Women*, John Wiley & Sons, 2001, p. 31.
16 Published by Church House Publishing for the General Synod; also available on the Ministry Division website: www.cofe-ministry.org.uk
17 Pamela Darling, *The Participation of Women in the Episcopal Church*, summary paper produced by Committee on the Status of Women, The Episcopal Church USA, 2003, p. 1.
18 'Leading with wisdom, compassion and patience: an interview with Molly Marshall', *Mutuality*, Spring 05, p. 6.
19 In particular, Resolution B, which prevents a woman being incumbent, priest in charge or team vicar in the benefice.
20 See Katie Brazelton, *Praying for Purpose for Women*, Zondervan, 2005, and related books.
21 See, for example, Dan B. Allender, *To be Told: Know Your Story, Shape Your Future*, Waterbrook Press, 2005.
22 Rick Warren, *The Purpose-Driven Life*, Zondervan, 2002, chs. 30–32.
23 Stacy Blake-Beard, 'The inextricable link between mentoring and leadership' in Coughlin et al. (eds.), *Enlightened Power*, p. 109.
24 Further details about Action Learning Sets are available from 3D Coaching, a coaching/training agency: www.3dcoaching.com.

25 John Mallison, *Mentoring to Develop Disciples and Leaders*, SU/ Open Book, 1998, p. 39.

26 Personal correspondence to the author.

27 One suggestion of how to find a mentor is to write to about six trusted friends, setting out the sort of mentor you are looking for, and asking them to pray and suggest people.

28 Robyn Claydon, Women Mentoring Women website, found via www.pastornet.net.au/chmentor/women.html.

29 Kelly Bean, 'Dancing toward equality in the emerging church', *Mutuality*, Fall 04, p. 12.

Conclusion

1 Danielle Strickland, 'Developing women', *Youthwork*, August 2007, p. 18.

Resource Section

1 If you are aged 25–40 you may be interested in the Arrow Leadership Programme: www.cpas.org.uk/arrow.

2 Awesome (see www.awesome.org.uk) is a support network for evangelical Anglican women who are ordained as priests or deacons.

GROWING LEADERS

Reflections on leadership, life and Jesus

JAMES LAWRENCE

Seven out of ten Christian leaders feel overworked, four in ten suffer financial pressures, only two in ten have had management training, and 1500 give up their job over a ten-year period. At the same time, as financial restrictions affect the availability of full-time ministers, more people are needed for leadership roles in local congregations for every area of church work.

This book faces the challenge of raising up new leaders and helping existing leaders to mature, using the model for growing leaders at the heart of the Arrow Leadership Programme, a ministry of the Church Pastoral Aid Society (CPAS). It comprehensively surveys leadership skills and styles, discerning our personal calling, avoiding the 'red zone' of stress, developing character, and living as part of the community of God's people.

ISBN 978 1 84101 246 9   £8.99
Available from your local Christian bookshop or, in case of difficulty, direct from BRF using the order form on page 239.

THE FOURFOLD LEADERSHIP OF JESUS

Come, follow, wait, go

ANDREW WATSON

'Don't follow me. Follow Jesus!' runs a popular slogan. The apostle Paul wrote, 'Follow my example, as I follow the example of Christ.' As leaders and would-be leaders, can we ever hope to echo Paul's words—or should we only point away from ourselves to Jesus? *The Fourfold Leadership of Jesus* explores what it means to lead as Jesus led, as he called his disciples to come, to follow, to wait, and to go.

These four commands embody the four different aspects of leadership that this book explores as a model for us today, a biblical alternative to the current popularity of management theories. As we follow Jesus we are transformed by the Holy Spirit into the likeness of Christ. Disciples are raised up as leaders, who in turn nurture further disciples, so that the work of the kingdom of God continues to grow, and we too can dare to echo Paul's bold words.

ISBN 978 1 84101 435 7 £7.99
Available from your local Christian bookshop or, in case of difficulty, direct from BRF using the order form on page 239.

COLLABORATIVE MINISTRY

What it is, how it works and why

DAVID ROBERTSON

'Collaborative ministry' is fast becoming a buzz phrase in the church, following on from phrases such as 'every-member ministry' and 'the priesthood of all believers'. It appears in ordination services and is used by churches advertising for a new minister. It is referred to by those who speak and write about leadership, the Church and outreach. It will, apparently, halt the decline in church leadership and also stimulate congregational growth. But what exactly does it mean? And does it fit with existing leadership structures?

This book sets out to define collaborative ministry. It comprehensively explores the theology and practice of this style of 'being church', considering the implications for churches both large and small. A central section provides foundational Bible studies, unpacking the themes of authority, acceptance and covenant, while an appendix of photocopiable group study material offers help for churches considering a collaborative approach.

ISBN 978 1 84101 493 7   £8.99
Available from your local Christian bookshop or, in case of difficulty, direct from BRF using the order form on page 239.

AN EMERGENT THEOLOGY
FOR EMERGING CHURCHES

RAY S. ANDERSON

This book explores the parallels between challenges facing the Church today and the first-century Antioch church, where Paul shaped 'emergent theology', developing from the 'parent' Jerusalem church. This was not a different gospel but a rigorous appraisal of what constituted the core of the message of salvation, as opposed to mere cultural and religious conventions. Paul's New Testament writings demonstrate this Spirit-filled framework of belief that enabled the Christian message to spread across the world.

At a time when there is much talk of 'emerging/mission-shaped church', Ray Anderson's book is a challenge to 'think theologically' and ensure that all such initiatives are rooted in a dynamic, transformative and biblically informed faith. It is essential reading for visionary church leaders, those training future leaders, and all concerned about presenting the gospel message in a fast-changing culture.

ISBN 978 1 84101 535 4   £8.99
Available from your local Christian bookshop or, in case of difficulty, direct from BRF using the order form on page 239.

SPIRITED WOMEN

Encountering the first women believers

MARY ELLEN ASHCROFT

Spirited Women is an invitation to travel across time and space in order to encounter lost relatives in the Christian faith. Set during the time of the book of Acts, just after the death of Stephen the first martyr, it explores the stories of some of the women involved in the early Church—Mary Magdalene, Martha, Mary the mother of Jesus, and Joanna, among others.

Drawing on the author's theological and historical research, biblical study and imagination, this book brings vivid life to women who have been largely forgotten or marginalized over the years. Exploring their experiences and their resilient faith, we too can be challenged and empowered in our walk with God. *Spirited Women* also includes questions that can be used for group or individual study, notes for further reading, and a detailed bibliography.

ISBN 978 1 84101 443 2   £6.99
Available from your local Christian bookshop or, in case of difficulty, direct from BRF using the order form on page 239.